PAINTING
Country
Cottages
&
Gardens

PAINTING
Country
Cottages
&
Gardens

Diane Trierweiler

NORTH LIGHT BOOKS
CINCINNATI, OHIO
www.nlbooks.com

Dedication

I would like to dedicate this book to my husband, Gilbert, and to my two children, Jared and Jami. Your loving encouragement and help while I have pursued my career has been much appreciated.

Thank you, Gil, for all of the conventions you have helped me with and for all of the creative input you have offered me. Thank you for fifteen wonderful years.

Acknowledgments

Many thanks to Dian, Debbie, Linda and Jane for helping me in my shop while I work on painting new projects and travel to teach them.

Thank you Van and Roland for providing interesting woodcuts for me to paint. Thanks also to Kathy Kipp of North Light Books for asking me to work with her company.

Painting Country Cottages and Gardens. Copyright © 2000 by Diane Trierweiler. Manufactured in China. All rights reserved. The patterns and drawings in this book are for the personal use of the decorative painter. By permission of the author and publisher, they may be either hand-traced or photocopied to make single copies, but under no circumstances may they be resold or republished. It is permissible for the purchaser to paint the designs contained herein and sell them at fairs, bazaars and craft shows. No other part of this book may be reproduced in any form or by any electronic or mechanical means including information storage and retrieval systems without permission in writing from the publisher, except by a reviewer, who may quote brief passages in a review. Published by North Light Books, an imprint of F&W Publications, Inc., 1507 Dana Avenue, Cincinnati, Ohio 45207. (800) 289-0963. First edition.

Other fine North Light Books are available from your local bookstore, art supply store or direct from the publisher.

04 03 02 01 00   5 4 3 2 1

Library of Congress Cataloging-in-Publication Data
Trierweiler, Diane
     Painting country cottages & gardens / Diane Trierweiler.
         p. cm.
     Includes index.
     ISBN 0-89134-996-0 (pbk. : alk. paper)
     ISBN 1-58180-065-7 (pob. : alk. paper)
      1. Painting. 2. Decoration and ornament. 3. Cottages in art. 4. Gardens in art. I. Title:
   Painting country cottages and gardens. II. Title.

TT385 .T75 2000
745.7'23—dc21   99-089907

Editor: Jennifer Long
Production Coordinator: Sara Dumford
Cover and interior designed by: Mary Barnes Clark
Photography by: Al Parrish and Christine Polomsky

About the Author

Diane Trierweiler began painting in 1980, teaching herself to paint in both watercolor and oils. It was not until her husband, Gil, encouraged her to take a decorative painting class that she became interested in the decorative painting field. After her first class, Diane said that she would one day open a decorative painting store. In 1986 her prediction came true, and The Tole Bridge opened its doors in Norco, California. Today, Diane teaches decorative painting throughout the U.S. and Canada. She and her husband love to travel, and teaching painting has afforded them the perfect opportunity to do this.

Diane works in many different styles, using oils, acrylics and watercolor. She is best known for her loosely stroked, vibrant paintings of flowers and landscapes. Diane encourages her students to use only minimal pattern lines and to make the designs their own. She also teaches color theory throughout her classes to encourage her students to become more independent in their painting.

Diane has been a member of the Society of Decorative Painters since 1985. She has published two books, *Diane Paints Victorian Treasures* and *Country Lane Flower Shop*. She has also produced almost one hundred pattern packets and four videos for the Perfect Palette Studio. Diane was born in Wisconsin, but has lived most of her life in southern California. Here she has found many wonderful students and friends in the decorative art field.

She has two grown children, Jami and Jared.

Table of Contents

Projects

Chapter 3
Step-by-Step Projects 22

Introduction

I think the best thing about decorative painting is that it offers patterns for people to use when painting a design. This gives people that would not have attempted painting on their own a chance to find that hidden talent they may not have known they had. From patterned work they can branch out into other areas, such as freehand strokework.

I try to encourage my students to use the basic structure of a pattern, but to create their own style in doing so. For instance, if you copy the basic structure of a rose from the pattern, try painting it in different colors or on different backgrounds or transform it into a different type of rose to create a rose that looks entirely different.

This works just as well with landscapes. Try changing the time of day of the scene you are painting. Changing the colors of the houses or the plants around them can give the whole scene a different feel. Make it your own.

Most of the things that I paint, whether they are formal or country, are reminiscent of the Victorian era. I love the way the Victorians decorated their homes and paid much attention to detail. Even the smallest objects in their homes were ornate and detailed. If I am painting something with a country feel, I usually include some lettering taken from advertisement art in the early 1900s.

I also love to paint stroke flowers. The time you put into practicing strokework will pay off in the end. Once you have mastered the basic strokes, there are so many things you can do with them. Strokework opens a whole world of creative expression and design. Decorating the walls of your home or a small piece of furniture can be so rewarding.

I hope you find the satisfaction and joy in painting that I have!

CHAPTER 1

GETTING STARTED

Paints

Acrylic paints are simply pigments suspended in water and resin. When applied to an object, the water evaporates, leaving the pigment and resin in place.

Curing time for acrylics is about seven days (this is also true for water-based varnishes). Unlike watercolor and gouache, once the acrylic is dry and cured, it will not move.

I use DecoArt Americana acrylics. The intensity of many of the DecoArt acrylic colors creates the look of an oil painting. Even when water is added to these acrylics, the pigments remain strong.

Palette

I like to lay my paints out on sheets of deli wrap with a moistened shop towel or a shop sponge underneath. The bright blue color of the shop towels under the deli wrap helps me to see my colors better.

To set up your palette, soak a shop towel or shop sponge in clean water. Lay this onto your palette. Lay a piece of deli wrap over the wet towel. The water will go through the deli wrap and keep your paints moist for a long time. Keep the towel or sponge wet by adding water to it now and then.

You can also blend your colors on the deli wrap without fear of picking

up dried specks of paint.

Even though the paints will stay wet a lot longer on the wet palette, I only squeeze out a small portion of paint at a time.

Painting Supplies

Shop towels are also good for absorbing the excess water from your brushes. They have very little lint, which prevents lint from transferring onto your work. The Loew-Cornell water tub has a partition in the middle to separate your clean and dirty water. A palette knife will be needed to mix your paints, although often paints are brush mixed.

Brushes

There are many brands and styles of brushes. Whatever brand you prefer, look for a quality golden Taklon brush. Taklon holds up better when using acrylic paints. You may prefer a mixed-bristle brush such as the Loew-Cornell Mixtique. These are made of half natural hair and half Taklon so they hold more water.

Fans and Mist Brushes

I like to use a natural-hair brush when painting trees and flowers in a landscape. The texture produced is softer and more muted than with a synthetic brush.

For this reason, I have designed Diane's Angel Series brushes. These are natural-hair short fan and mist brushes in a variety of sizes for painting foliage and flowers. They are available exclusively from The Tole Bridge, 1875 Norco Drive, Norco, CA 91760. Phone (909) 272-6918.

Angle Brushes

I prefer to shade with an angle brush. Angle brushes are more comfortable to tip when you need to go into smaller areas. You should be able to use a large angle to paint just about everything.

When painting stroke roses, angle brushes help you to pull your strokes along more comfortably. I like to work with Loew-Cornell angle brushes.

Filberts

When I am painting stroke flowers, I usually use a filbert brush. These brushes come in sizes 10/0 to ½ inch (1.3cm). Filberts don't leave stop-and-start edges. Stroke leaves and

Some of My Brushes

Shown from top to bottom are Diane's script liner, Loew-Cornell series 7500 filbert, Loew-Cornell series 7400 angle, Loew-Cornell series 7300 flat, Diane's Angel Hair, Diane's Angel Mist, Diane's Angel Wing, Loew-Cornell series 275 mop and Loew-Cornell series 798 glazing brush.

flowers are easy to form because of the round edges of the bristles.

The ½-inch (1.3cm) filbert is also wonderful to scumble in skies or faux finishes.

Flats

Flat brushes are good for basecoating areas. They come in a range of sizes from 10/0 to two inch (5.1cm).

Liners

Loew-Cornell makes many sizes of liner brushes. For very fine lines, you may use an 18/0. Generally, though, a good 10/0 script liner is what I use.

Liner brushes can be used to pull comma strokes. The more hairs a brush has, the longer the distance before reloading.

Brush Care

I always keep two Loew-Cornell brush tubs full of clean water next to me; constantly rinsing your brushes in dirty water will ruin them quickly.

Once I have thoroughly rinsed my brush, I always squeeze the water out of the bristles and reshape the chisel edge. Then I lay it down flat on a paper towel as I continue to paint. This keeps any dirty water from flowing up into the ferrule.

At the end of the painting session, I use DecoMagic brush cleaner to clean my acrylic brushes. Be sure to rinse the cleaner out of the brush before you paint again.

A good brush case is also necessary. Use one that opens up so that you can reach for your brushes without bending all of the other brush bristles. With proper care, your brushes should last a long time.

Choosing and Preparing Your Surfaces ❧

I first started painting with oils on canvas. The decorative art field opened up a whole new world of surfaces on which to express my creative abilities: tin, ceramic, wood, paper, papier maché, glass, etc. I also have come to enjoy painting on rustic wood pieces. Little preparation is needed, and the old barn wood lends interest to the design.

If you prefer painting on smooth surfaces, be sure to check each wood piece for flaws and cracks before purchasing it. You will spend a lot less time in preparation if your wood has been well cut.

Taking time to prepare your surface before painting is very important. Follow the simple steps below to get the best results.

Wood

1. First, fill nail holes and imperfections in the surface with J.W. etc. Wood Filler. Then use a fine-grit sanding disc to lightly sand the wood before sealing.

2. Apply J.W. etc. First Step Wood Sealer with a large glazing brush. You may also use a sponge brush. I prefer to seal the surface that I will be painting first, then wait for a week or two to seal and basecoat the back or inside of the surface. This gives any moisture still left in the wood time to dry out, rather than being trapped inside the piece.

If you have time to wait for an oil-based sealer to dry, I recommend McCloskey oil sealer. If you wish to paint shortly after sealing, use a water-based sealer.

3. To save time, mix equal amounts of paint and sealer for your first basecoat, then use full-strength paint for the second coat. When basecoating, always aim for smooth, even coverage.

4. After each layer of paint, you will notice the grain of the wood rising. This happens because you have added moisture to your surface. Lightly sand the surface after each layer and wipe clean with a tack cloth. Some woods have wider grains that tend to raise more. If this is the case with your piece, you may want to use gesso in place of wood sealer. It will help to fill the grain.

Bisque

When painting on bisque, lightly sand the surface until smooth, then wipe clean with a tack cloth.

If you will be using the bisque piece to hold liquids or food, be sure to ask the dealer to glaze the inside. This is an inexpensive process and makes your piece functional.

Tinware

Before painting tinware, you will need to wash the surface with soap and water. The manufacturer often leaves an oily residue on the tin that will not allow your paint to adhere. Be sure to dry the tinware thoroughly after washing so that it doesn't rust.

I like to use a gray primer spray on tin before I paint to give the surface tooth and to help seal it.

Canvas

Canvas is a nice surface for painters. Usually the canvas has been pre-gessoed and is ready to paint on. I prefer portrait-quality, stretched polyester canvas. It is smooth and bounces back if dented.

Other Surfaces

Scouring a flea market or garage sale can produce many inexpensive and interesting surfaces to paint on—old purses, suitcases, furniture, glassware, etc. The choices of surfaces are almost endless and, after all, variety is the spice of life.

Faux Finishes ❧

If I am not painting a landscape, I love to use faux finishes as the background for the design. Apply the paint with a sea sponge to make color variations for a simple finish.

The sea sponge already has irregular holes in it and is round, so you won't get even patterns of color. Always pre-wet your sponge before using.

There are many ways to faux finish. Try applying the paint with feathers, rags, doilies, paper towels and other interesting textures to get the right effect. Just using your fingers or the edge of your palm creates a great texture over wet paint.

Transferring the Patterns ❧

1. Use a photocopier to enlarge or reduce the pattern you wish to paint to fit your project surface.

2. Place tracing paper over the pattern. Use a sharp pencil to trace all of the major lines. The small detail lines are for your visual reference and don't need to be transferred.

3. Place the tracing over your prepared surface and tape in place.

4. I rarely use graphite to transfer a pattern—it tends to smear and show through the paint. Super Chacopa-

per is water washable and much easier to work with. Slip the Super Chacopaper under the tracing. Use a stylus to trace over the basic pattern lines. I use white Saral paper to transfer patterns onto dark backgrounds.

When you transfer your design to the surface, use as little patterning as possible. Your pattern won't be as confusing to follow, and your painting will look more natural.

Varnishing

There are many ways to varnish. DecoArt Matte Spray DAS13 is nice for some projects, but generally a brush-on varnish covers better and more quickly. I use J.W. etc. Right-Step Satin Varnish, applied with a ¾-inch (1.9cm) glazing brush. Between coats of varnish, gently resand the piece and wipe with a tack cloth.

Gold Leafing

Gold leafing is simple to do. It's just a little messy. You will need gold leaf, gold leaf adhesive, matte spray and acrylic antiquing gel. See project seven, page 89 for step-by-step instructions.

Spattering

1. To spatter, varnish the piece first so that you can wipe unwanted spatters away easily.

2. Thin the paint slightly with water.

3. Fill an Angel Wing brush completely with paint and gently tap the brush ferrule with another brush. Make a few test spatters on paper before you do the entire piece.

You can also use a toothbrush loaded with paint, then scrape a palette knife over it to create spatters. Spattering is also used in project seven on page 89.

Antiquing

1. Always varnish the piece before applying antiquing. This will keep the antiquing medium from going so deeply into the grain of the wood that you can't rub it out.

2. Apply antiquing medium to the surface and wipe the excess off until you are satisfied with the color.

3. Varnish when dry. Antiquing medium is also great for floating color on.

Painting Procedure

Following are a few suggestions to help you paint the projects in this book.

1. Prepare and basecoat the piece as directed on page 12.

2. Apply the pattern to the larger areas, then basecoat these areas. This should be done with smooth, opaque coverage.

3. Next, transfer the pattern details and paint these smaller areas. Begin by floating the shading on and then adding the highlights.

4. The detailing is next. After this is completed, the shading may be deepened and the highlights raised as needed.

5. After painting, let the piece dry for a few days, then varnish. For the best results, use at least three coats of varnish.

Some designs in this book are done with freehand strokework. The patterns for these designs are provided strictly as a reference. It is much easier to paint strokework without a transferred pattern. You can do it!

Paint all of these designs with opaque colors, except in the few instances where a wash of color is called for.

CHAPTER 2

BASIC TECHNIQUES

Side Loading Your Brush

To side load, first dip a flat or angle brush into water. Touch one corner of the brush into paint and work the brush back and forth on your palette until a nice progression of color is attained, with dark color on one side and water on the other.

1 Dip your brush into water and blot on a paper towel. Pick up a tiny bit of paint on the corner of your brush.

2 Blend your brush in both directions on your palette.

3 Move slightly into the color using very little pressure. Keep your hand in the middle of the brush handle when you begin to float a color. Shadows become softer if you stay back on your brush handle.

Double Loading

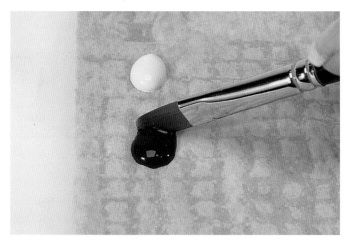

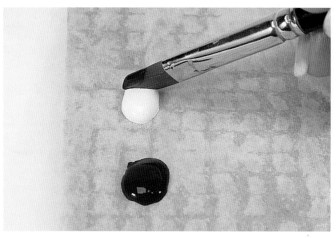

1 Turn your brush on its side and load into one color.

2 Turn your brush on its other side and load into a second color.

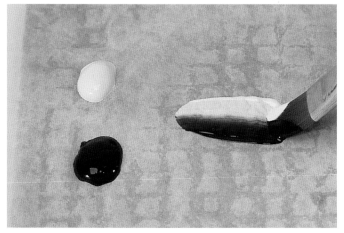

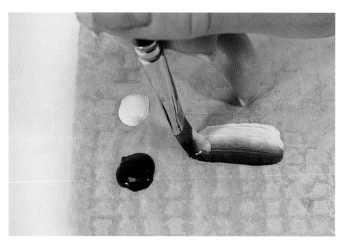

3 Blend on your palette.

4 Reverse direction and blend again. Keep the dark side of the brush on the dark side of the stroke.

One-Stroke Leaves and Petals

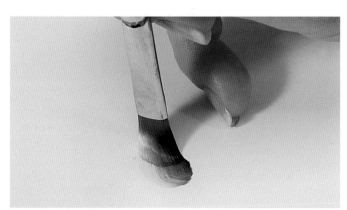

5 To make a one-stroke figure, press the whole flat edge of your double-loaded brush down. Begin turning your brush and lifting as you move. These strokes may be painted singly or with two side-by-side strokes for leaves and flowers.

6 Raise the brush completely onto its chisel edge and pull away.

Double Loading an Angel Wing Brush

1 Dip half of your brush into one color of paint.

2 Dip the other half of your brush into a second color.

3 Pounce your brush out on the palette so that the colors blend in the middle, but don't completely mix.

4 Press the Angel Wing bristles down on the palette and twist back and forth to flay them out.

5 Tip back and forth on the edge of your bristles to gently add dark and light colors to your surface. Roll back on the dark edge for dark areas and roll up on the light edge for the lightest areas.

Dabbing

Hold the brush perpendicular to the surface of the board and make short, stabbing strokes to the surface.

Stippling

Use Diane's Angel Mist brush. Dip into paint and pounce out on your palette. Lightly touch down on the surface in a tapping motion. Every time you add a color, use less color and less pressure.

Double-Loaded Stippling

1 To paint a double-loaded stipple, dip one side of your brush into one color.

2 Dip the other side of your brush into a second color.

3 Pounce your brush out on the palette so that the colors blend in the middle but don't completely mix.

4 Fill in the area with a tapping motion.

Painting a Wash

A wash is created when color is thinned with water, Winsor & Newton Acrylic Flow Improver or textile medium until it is almost transparent.

Apply this mix over a painted area to change the underlying color slightly, or base an unpainted area with a wash for a transparent effect.

Shading and Highlighting with Floated Color

Shading and highlighting add definition to a painted piece. I add my shades and highlights with a "floated-color" technique.

To float color, simply dip a flat or angle brush in water and blot the excess water out by touching the brush to a paper towel. (Some water should remain in the brush.)

Side load the brush by touching one corner of the bristles to a puddle of paint, then stroke the brush back and forth in the same spot on the palette, until the paint has begun to move across the bristles (see page 14).

Keeping the brush flat on the surface, apply the color side to the darker edge of the area to be shaded.

To reload, thoroughly rinse the brush and repeat the procedure.

1 To create a wash, add water to your paint so that you can see your palette through the paint. This usually takes a half-and-half mix of paint and water.

2 When painting a washed leaf, work back and forth on the chisel edge of your brush. This will create little pockets of texture or dark and light.

Floating
Side load your brush into a darker (for shading) or lighter (for highlighting) color and float the color along the edges of an area, such as this leaf.

Tinting

Tinting is done very lightly with floated or washed color. It is just a hint of color reflection used to create interest and harmony—for example, tinting the edge of a leaf with the flower color or tinting a house with some of the flower colors that surround it.

Wet-on-Wet

This technique is used when you are stippling or dabbing colors on the surface while the undercolor is still wet. Start with your darkest colors and progress to the lightest colors.

Each time you add a color, use less pressure on your brush and less color. Let enough of your darker color show through to create shadows.

Scumbling

Scumbling is a term used to describe the pattern of brushstrokes on a surface. I like to use a filbert brush to scumble because the edges of the colors blend together better with this brush.

You will develop your own pattern the more you use this technique. I use this method in painting skies quite often.

1 To paint wet-on-wet, first paint in small areas of color one at a time.

2 While the first color is still wet, add a second color over the first. Use very little pressure.

1 To scumble, completely load your brush with color. Move back and forth in an **X**.

2 While your first color is still wet add a second color, moving back and forth in **X**-strokes.

Painting Straw with an Angel Hair Brush *

Painting with Diane's Angel Hair brush is like using many liners at once.

1 Load the brush with color, adding water to your paint as you do this. Flatten the brush to get the excess paint out.

2 Stay up on the tips of the bristles as you pull tiny lines.

Painting Grass *

1 Add water to your paint so that you can see your palette through the paint. This usually requires a half-and-half mix of paint and water.

2 Place your Angel Wing brush down on the ends of the bristles and pull down.

Linework

1 Add water to your paint and load the liner brush almost to the ferrule.

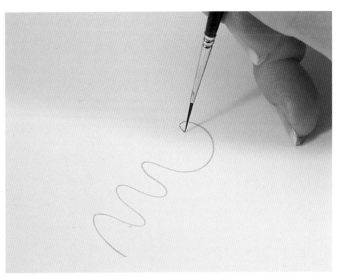

2 Spin the brush to a point. Stay up on the tip of the brush when painting.

Painting Dots with Your Liner Brush

These dots are useful for painting flower seeds and centers. When you paint something that is alive, you will create a more natural look if you use the ends of your liner brush bristles instead of a stylus. The brush bristles will create a more abstract shape. Dot your brush into the color and tap it lightly into the centers of your flowers.

CHAPTER 3

STEP-BY-STEP PROJECTS

Forget-Me-Not Candy Dish

This pretty little glass dish with a wooden lid is perfect for candy or small trinkets. The beginning painter should be able to accomplish this small design easily.

If you relax and keep your hand in the middle of your brush handle, your design will be loose and free-flowing. Tiny dabs of a double-loaded brush will create the look of a French Victorian design.

Preparation

1. Fill, sand and seal the wooden lid. Use your ¾-inch (1.9cm) glazing brush and Light Buttermilk to base the entire lid. You will need to use two to three coats for good coverage.

2. Basecoat the outer edge of the lid with Emperor's Gold. This should come over the rounded edge.

3. Transfer the pattern for the blue band. Base this band with Blue Chiffon.

4. When the lid is dry, transfer the pattern for flowers. Use as few lines as possible for a more freehand look.

Materials

DecoArt Americana Acrylic Paints

Titanium White DA1	Boysenberry Pink DA29	Victorian Blue DA39	Williamsburg Blue DA40	Avocado DA52	Hauser Light Green DA131
Light Buttermilk DA164	Blue Chiffon DA193	Violet Haze DA197			

DecoArt Dazzling Metallics

Emperor's Gold DA148

Surface

This lovely candy dish and many others may be purchased from Jo C. and Co., 111 Parrish Lane, Wilmington, Delaware 19810-3457. Phone (302) 478-7619.

Loew-Cornell Brushes

- series 798 ¾-inch (1.9cm) glazing brush
- series 7050 10/0 liner (or Diane's 10/0 script liner)
- series 7300 ½-inch (1.3cm) angle
- series 7500 no. 2 filbert

Miscellaneous

- J.W. etc. Wood Filler
- fine sanding disc
- J.W. etc. First Step Wood Sealer
- tracing paper and pencil
- Chacopaper
- Kemper stylus
- Winsor & Newton Acrylic Flow Improver
- J.W. etc. Right-Step Satin Varnish

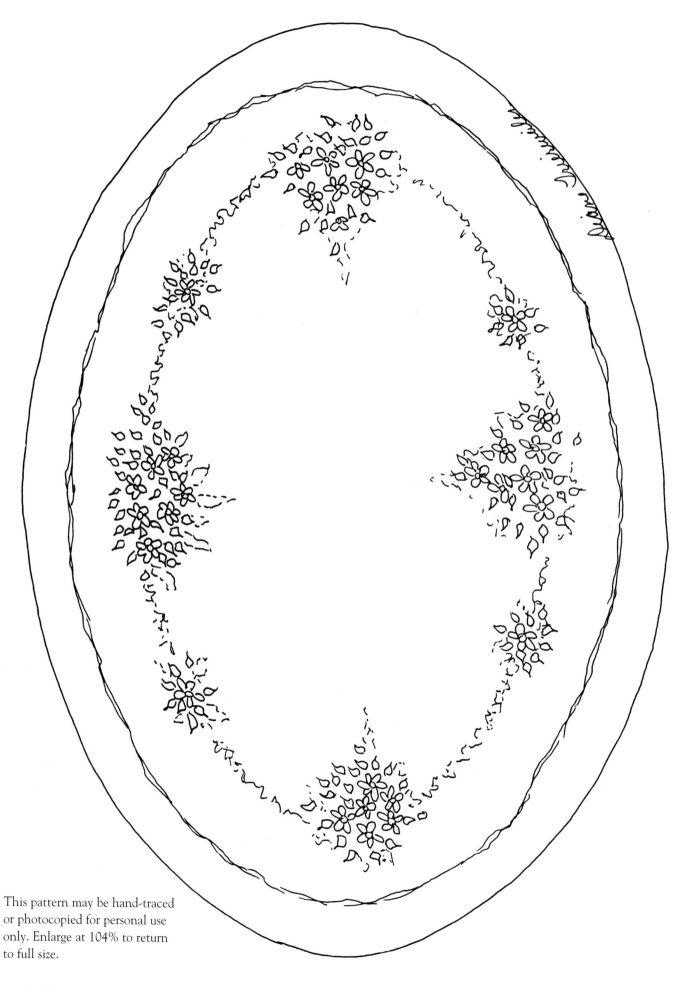

This pattern may be hand-traced or photocopied for personal use only. Enlarge at 104% to return to full size.

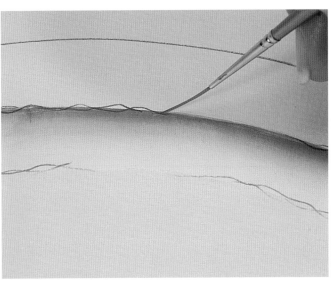

1 Use your ½-inch (1.3cm) angle brush to float a shadow of Williamsburg Blue onto the Blue Chiffon band. (See page 18 for instructions on floating color.)

2 Use your liner brush loaded with Avocado to line in the vine around the Blue Chiffon band. (See page 21 for instructions on linework.)

3 Double load your no. 2 filbert with Victorian Blue and Titanium White. Stroke on one-stroke petals (page 15). Give some flowers two petals, some three petals and some five petals. Also stroke a few separate petals here and there.

4 To make the leaves, use your no. 2 filbert loaded with Hauser Light Green and water. Press down on your brush to begin the leaf, then pull up to a point to make the tip.

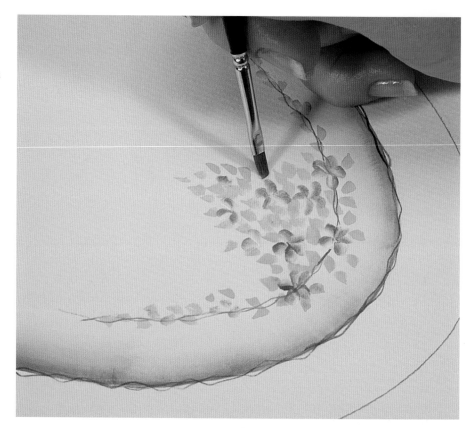

5 Repeat step four using Avocado to make more leaves. Use your liner brush and Avocado to make small stems and vein lines.

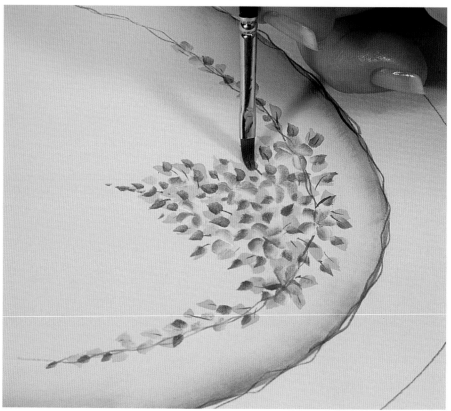

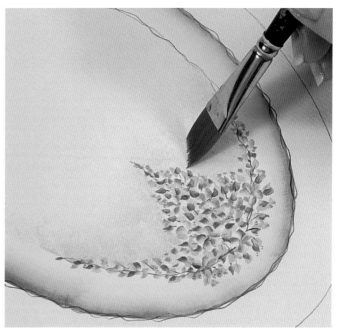

6 Use your liner brush loaded with Emperor's Gold to tap in the flower centers. To create filler flowers, add water to Violet Haze and gently tap them in with the chisel edge of your no. 2 filbert brush. Use your no. 2 filbert brush and Boysenberry Pink to tap in tiny filler dots.

7 Use your glazing brush to dampen the center area with Winsor & Newton Acrylic Flow Improver. Use a ½-inch (1.3cm) angle brush to float Boysenberry Pink around the flower design. As you begin to float color around the design, pick your brush up and pull color toward the inner area of the design. Gently soften as you move along. The flow improver will level out the paint as you touch the brush down.

8 Finish the piece by varnishing with at least two coats of J.W. etc. Right-Step Satin Varnish.

Cottage Music Box

This small music box can be accomplished easily by painters of all skill levels. It would make a lovely addition to any home.

Most people are fascinated by music boxes, as I am. I have brought together my love of Tudor cottages and music boxes in this project.

Preparation

1. Fill, sand and seal your wood. Transfer the pattern.

2. Base in the design as follows: Base the sky with Soft Blue. Base the house walls with Sand. Base the chimney and door with Heritage Brick. Base the windows with a wash of Burnt Umber. Base the grass with a wash of Hauser Medium Green (use half paint and half water). Base the roof with Honey Brown.

3. When these areas are dry, transfer the rest of your pattern.

Materials

DecoArt Americana Acrylic Paints

Titanium
White DA1

Sand
DA4

Cadmium Yellow
DA10

Sea Aqua
DA46

Olive Green
DA56

Burnt Umber
DA64

Lamp Black
DA67

Dioxazine Purple
DA101

Light Cinnamon
DA114

Hauser Medium
Green DA132

Hauser Dark Green
DA133

Honey Brown
DA163

Violet Haze
DA197

Primary Blue
DA200

Soft Blue
DA210

Peony Pink
DA215

Heritage Brick
DA219

Surface

If you don't have a local woodcutter who can cut this piece for you, you may purchase the wood piece from The Tole Bridge, 1875 Norco Drive, Norco, California 91760. Phone (909) 272-6918.

Loew-Cornell Brushes

- series 7050 10/0 liner
- series 7300 no. 1, no. 4 and no. 10 flats
- series 7400 ½-inch (1.3cm) angle

Diane's Angel Series Brushes

- Diane's Angel Mist brush, ⅜-inch (1cm)
- Diane's Angel Hair brush, ½-inch (1.3cm)

Materials list continued on page 31.

This pattern may be hand-traced or photocopied for personal use only. Enlarge at 185% to return to full size.

1 Basecoat and reapply the design as instructed on page 29. Use your liner brush and Burnt Umber to line in some tree branches behind the cottage. Add water to a little Violet Haze and use your Angel Mist brush to stipple (see page 17) foliage on the trees—this will represent trees in the far distance. Repeat this step using Hauser Medium Green, then Hauser Dark Green. When dry, highlight the leaves with a stipple of Olive Green. Stipple one last highlight on the tips of the trees with a mix of Olive Green plus Titanium White. Use your angle brush to float a shadow of Hauser Dark Green into the unpainted halo between the house and trees. Use your no. 4 flat brush and Light Cinnamon to base in the timbers on the front of the house. Use your no. 1 flat brush and Light Cinnamon to begin adding small bricks on the walls.

Materials *continued*

Miscellaneous

- J.W. etc. Wood Filler
- fine sanding disc
- J.W. etc. First Step Wood Sealer
- tracing paper and pencil
- Chacopaper
- Kemper stylus
- J.W. etc. Right-Step Satin Varnish

2 When the bricks are dry, drybrush some Titanium White highlights onto the walls. Use your liner brush loaded with Titanium White to line in the window frames. Use your angle brush and Light Cinnamon to shade the walls where the roof overhangs and around the door and windows. Shade the bottom of each timber with Burnt Umber.

3 Use your angle brush and Violet Haze to shade over the shadow areas on the house—this will create a back-light. Also add Violet Haze shading on the darkest areas of the windows and their frames. Use the wet-on-wet method (page 19) to paint the door: Repaint the door with Heritage Brick. While this is still wet, add Sand plus Cadmium Yellow for highlights and Burnt Umber for shadows. When dry, shade the left side of the door with Lamp Black. Shade the darkest areas on the door with Violet Haze for a backlight.

4 Mix Heritage Brick plus Sand to get a light peach color. Use this color and your no. 1 flat to paint in small bricks on the chimney. Use your angle brush and Burnt Umber to shade the chimney. Float a highlight on the chimney with Heritage Brick plus Sand. Use Violet Haze to create a backlight in the shadow areas on the chimney. Add water to Light Cinnamon and stroke dark-colored straw on the roof with your Angel Hair brush. (See page 20 for this technique.) Repeat this step using Burnt Umber.

5 Add water to Cadmium Yellow. Use this color and your Angel Hair brush to add lighter straw to the roof. Repeat this step using Sand plus Cadmium Yellow. If another highlight is needed, use Cadium Yellow plus Titanium White. Tint the straw in the dark areas using Violet Haze and in the lighter areas using Sea Aqua. Tint the chimney in the light areas with Sea Aqua.

6 Base the steps and pathway with Sand. Use your angle brush to shade the steps with Burnt Umber. Highlight the steps with Titanium White, then tint them with Violet Haze. Shade the pathway with your angle brush and Burnt Umber. Highlight through the center of the path with Titanium White. Tint the path with Violet Haze.

7 Using your Angel Mist brush, stipple shrubs into the flower beds. Do this using Hauser Dark Green, Hauser Medium Green, Olive Green and Olive Green plus Titanium White. Stipple the lawn area with your Angel Mist brush, using Hauser Dark Green in the darkest areas and Olive Green in the lightest areas. Stipple the flowers wet-on-wet using various combinations of colors such as Dioxazine Purple and Titanium White, Cadmium Yellow and Titanium White, Peony Pink and Titanium White, Primary Blue and Titanium White and Sea Aqua and Titanium White. Use your liner brush to make sit-down flowers for daisies. To do this, load the tip of the brush with paint. Press the brush down on the side of the bristles. Pick the brush up and move on to the next petal. Make the centers Cadmium Yellow. Stipple in Cadmium Yellow, Peony Pink and Titanium White to make tall, coral flowers. Carry some flowers over onto the lawn area. Use your liner brush and Hauser Dark Green and Olive Green to line in small grass here and there. The above steps are shown completed on page 35.

8 Varnish with at least two coats of J. W. etc. Right-Step
  Satin Varnish. Install the music box.

English Tea

This is a functional teapot—it has been glazed inside so that you may serve hot tea from it. It would make a nice addition to your coffee table, especially if your home decor is Victorian.

I find that painting a small scene tends to go very quickly because you don't have to include as much detail as you do when painting a large scene. However, if you're feeling ambitious, you can enlarge this design and put it on a canvas or a piece of wood.

The faux finish on this teapot is quite simple.

Preparation

1. If your bisque piece feels a little rough, you may want to sand it lightly.
2. Use masking tape to tape off the area where the design will be.
3. Base the teapot with Antique Mauve, working around the taped-off area.

4. When dry, add water to a sea sponge and squeeze the excess water out. Tap the sponge into Deep Burgundy, then tap the excess paint onto your palette. With very light pressure, sponge over the Antique Mauve surface (see page 38).

5. When dry, remove the tape and transfer the basic design to the unpainted area, omitting the detail for now.

Materials

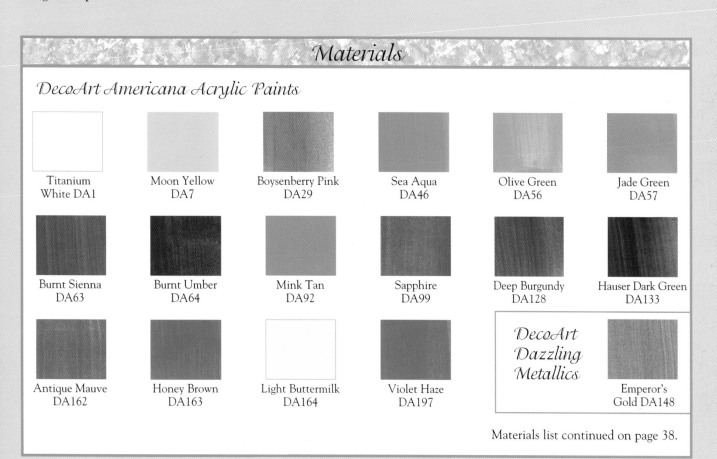

DecoArt Americana Acrylic Paints

Titanium White DA1	Moon Yellow DA7	Boysenberry Pink DA29	Sea Aqua DA46	Olive Green DA56	Jade Green DA57
Burnt Sienna DA63	Burnt Umber DA64	Mink Tan DA92	Sapphire DA99	Deep Burgundy DA128	Hauser Dark Green DA133
Antique Mauve DA162	Honey Brown DA163	Light Buttermilk DA164	Violet Haze DA197		

DecoArt Dazzling Metallics

Emperor's Gold DA148

Materials list continued on page 38.

This pattern may be hand-traced or photocopied for personal use only. Shown at full size.

Materials *continued*

Surface

This bisque teapot is available from Talk of the Town, 9000 Arlington Avenue #102, Riverside, California 92503. Phone (909) 687-4160.

Loew-Cornell Brushes
- series 7050 10/0 liner
- series 7300 no. 4 flat
- series 7400 ½-inch (1.3cm) angle
- series 7500 no. 6 filbert

Diane's Angel Series Brushes
- Diane's Angel Mist brush, ⅜-inch (1cm)
- Diane's Angel Hair brush, ⅜-inch (1cm)

Miscellaneous
- fine sanding disc
- masking tape
- sea sponge
- tracing paper and pencil
- Chacopaper
- Kemper stylus
- J.W. etc. Right-Step Satin Varnish

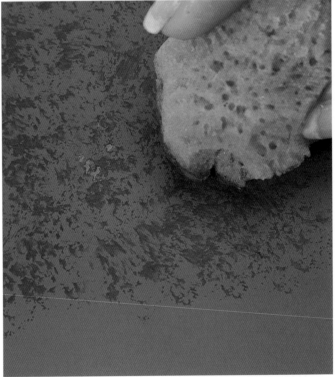

1 Always add water to your sea sponge when doing a faux finish. Lightly sponge over the basecoated area, making sure the undercolor shows through. Turn your sponge in different directions so that you don't create definite patterns in your finish.

2 Use your no. 6 filbert brush to scumble Titanium White and Sapphire into the sky area. Create a lot of texture on the surface.

3 Use your filbert brush to wash the path with a mix of half Mink Tan and half water. Use your angle brush to shade both sides of the path with Burnt Umber.

4 Use your filbert brush to wash in the lawn with a mix of half Jade Green and half water. Tint the center of the path with Boysenberry Pink. Tint the darkest areas of the path with Violet Haze. Drybrush a little Titanium White highlight through the center of the path.

5 Use your angle brush to shade the lawn with Hauser Dark Green. This should be done on the sides of the design, around the flower beds and path and horizontally through the center of the lawn. Wash in highlights through the center of the lawn with Olive Green.

6 Tint the light areas of the lawn with Boysenberry Pink. Tint the dark areas of the lawn with Violet Haze. Also add Violet Haze around the flower beds.

7 Tint the sky with small washes of Boysenberry Pink and then Sea Aqua. When this is dry, side load your angle brush with Light Buttermilk and float in clouds. Float highlights on the tops of the clouds using your angle brush and Titanium White. Be sure that you don't cover all of the Light Buttermilk.

8 Add water to Violet Haze and use your Angel Mist brush to stipple in where the trees will be. The violet color creates the illusion of trees far in the distance. Use your liner brush and Burnt Umber to line in tree branches and tree trunks.

9 Use your Angel Mist brush to lightly stipple the tree foliage in with Hauser Dark Green, Jade Green, Olive Green and Olive Green plus Titanium White. Each time you add a color, use less color and less pressure.

10 Base in the walls of the cottage with your no. 4 flat brush and Light Buttermilk. Use your liner brush and Burnt Umber to paint in the timbers on the house. Base the chimneys with your no. 4 flat brush and Burnt Sienna. Add water to Burnt Sienna and use your liner brush to paint tiny bricks on the walls. Shade the walls with your angle brush and Burnt Umber.

11 Base the roof with your no. 4 flat brush and Honey Brown. Use your Angel Hair brush to create straw on the roof; start by shading with Burnt Sienna. Add water to your paint to achieve an inklike consistency.

12 Add highlights to the roof using your Angel Hair brush and Moon Yellow, then Light Buttermilk. Shade one more time in the shadow areas with Burnt Umber.

13 Add water to Sapphire and wash this color inside the windows. Use your liner brush to paint in the window frames with Burnt Umber. Use your angle brush and Violet Haze to float backlight into the shadow areas on the walls. Base the door in with Burnt Sienna. Shade the door with your angle brush and Burnt Umber.

14 Mix Burnt Sienna plus Titanium White to make light bricks for the chimneys. Paint the bricks on with your liner brush. Shade the chimneys with your angle brush and Burnt Umber. Add backlight in the shadow areas with Violet Haze.

15 Use your Angel Mist brush to stipple greens into the flower beds. Use Hauser Dark Green, Jade Green and Olive Green.

16 After your greens are dry, use your Angel Mist brush to stipple in flowers, using various colors from your palette, such as Moon Yellow, Sapphire, Sea Aqua and Boysenberry Pink. This should be done wet-on-wet using Titanium White with these colors. Stipple a little Violet Haze into the flower beds to create shadows. The scene is now complete.

17 Use your liner brush to outline the design with Emperor's Gold. Line in a Titanium White band around the design and outline this line with Emperor's Gold. Varnish the entire piece with several coats of J. W. etc. Right-Step Satin Varnish.

Hydrangeas & Wildflowers

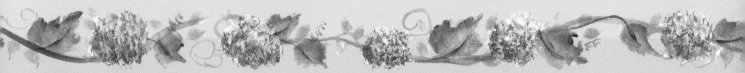

There are many uses for this lovely little piece of furniture and just as many uses for this floral design.

If you choose to scale the design down, it would look nice on a tray or small tabletop. It would also look nice over a doorway in your home or going up a wall in the corner; in this case you might leave the border design off and just use the flowers.

Once you have completed the trim, the design can be painted freehand and very loosely.

Preparation

1. Fill, sand and then paint the entire wood piece with a mixture of 80% J.W. etc. White Lightning plus 20% Light Buttermilk.

2. Mask off the border and base it with Soft Sage.

3. Remove the tape and transfer the pattern for the crosshatch lines.

4. Use your liner brush and Emperor's Gold plus a little water to line in the crosshatch pattern.

5. Let dry, then transfer the pattern for the rest of the design. Only minimal pattern lines are necessary.

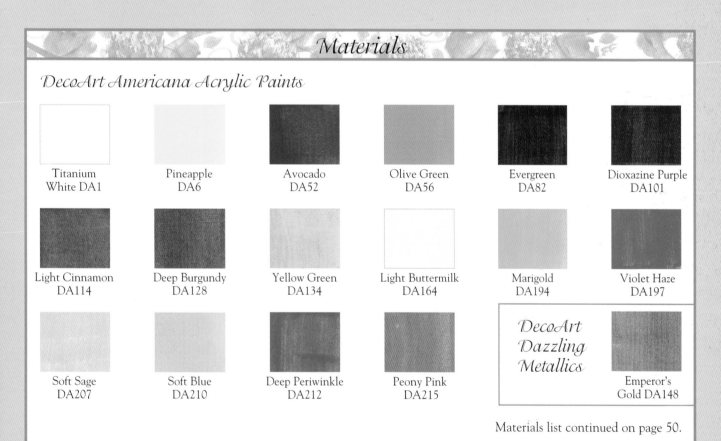

Materials

DecoArt Americana Acrylic Paints

Titanium White DA1	Pineapple DA6	Avocado DA52	Olive Green DA56	Evergreen DA82	Dioxazine Purple DA101
Light Cinnamon DA114	Deep Burgundy DA128	Yellow Green DA134	Light Buttermilk DA164	Marigold DA194	Violet Haze DA197
Soft Sage DA207	Soft Blue DA210	Deep Periwinkle DA212	Peony Pink DA215		

DecoArt Dazzling Metallics

Emperor's Gold DA148

Materials list continued on page 50.

pattern for top of chest

This pattern may be hand-traced or photocopied for personal
use only. Enlarge at 189% to return to full size.

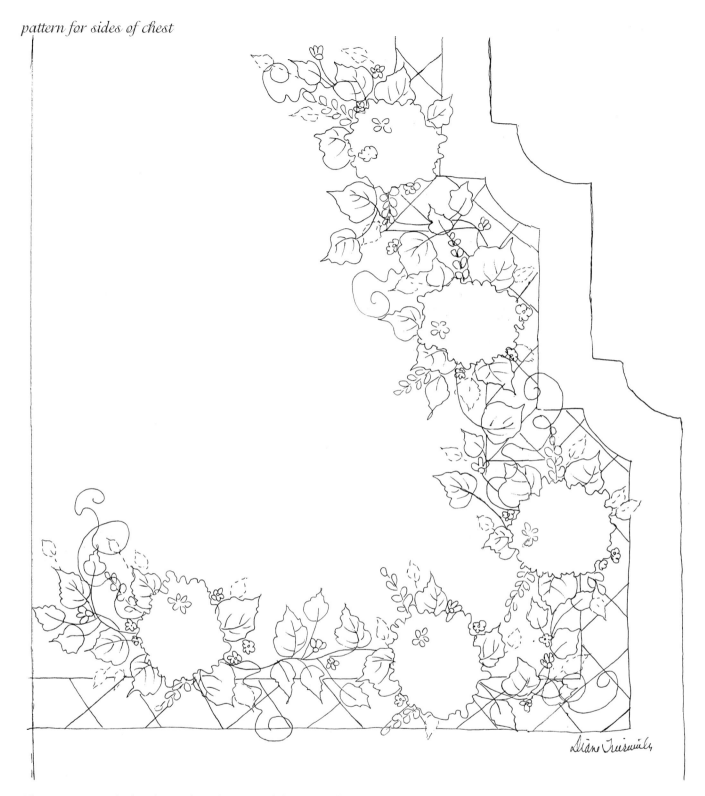

This pattern may be hand-traced or photocopied for personal use only. Enlarge at 189% to return to full size.

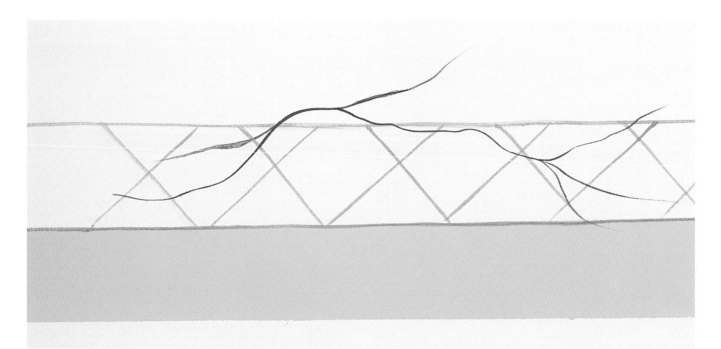

1 Use your flat brush to base the border trim with Soft Sage. Use your liner brush and Emperor's Gold to line in the crosshatch design. Make a half-and-half mix of Light Cinnamon and Avocado. Add water to the mix and use your liner brush to loosely line in the vines.

2 Add water to Avocado. Using your no. 10 filbert, stroke on transparent one-stroke leaves. Connect some leaves to the vine and leave some outside of the vine.

Materials *continued*

Surface

This three-drawer chest and many other great wooden pieces may be purchased wholesale from Roland Nimmo, 9198 Bonita Drive, Cherry Valley, California 92223. Phone (909) 845-6527.

You can also purchase the piece retail from The Tole Bridge, 1875 Norco Drive, Norco, California 91760. Phone (909) 272-6918.

Diane's Angel Series Brushes
• Diane's Angel Mist brush, ½-inch (1.3cm)

Loew-Cornell Brushes
• series 798 ¾-inch (1.9cm) glazing brush
• series 7050 10/0 liner
• series 7300 no. 10 flat
• series 7400 ⅜-inch (1cm) angle
• series 7500 no. 2, no. 4, no. 6 and no. 10 filberts

Miscellaneous
• J.W. etc. Wood Filler
• fine sanding disc
• J.W. etc. White Lightning
• masking tape
• tracing paper and pencil
• Chacopaper
• Kemper stylus
• J.W. etc. Right-Step Satin Varnish

3 Shade the leaves with Evergreen, using your angle brush. Paint the vein lines with your liner brush and Olive Green. Paint the tendrils with Evergreen.

4 Tint the leaves here and there with Deep Burgundy to create the look of color reflecting from your flowers. Tint again lightly with Yellow Green.

5 Double load your Angel Mist brush with Peony Pink and Deep Burgundy. Stipple in an irregular circle for each hydrangea.

6 While the stippled area is still wet, use your no. 2 filbert and Titanium White to stroke on tiny one-stroke florets. If your underpainting starts to dry, mix Titanium White with Peony Pink and continue stroking on the petals. Be sure that your small white strokes go over the outer edge of the circle you originally stippled. Use your liner brush to dot Olive Green centers in the florets.

7 Use your no. 10 filbert brush to shade around the bottoms of the flowers using Deep Burgundy. Dabble a little Violet Haze around the bottoms of the flowers.

8 To paint the blue filler flowers, double load your no. 6 filbert with Deep Periwinkle and Soft Blue. Stroke on one-stroke petals in a fern shape. Connect the petals with a line of Avocado.

9 To paint the yellow filler flowers, double load your no. 6 filbert with Pineapple and Marigold. Tap down on the chisel edge of your brush three times to create these flowers.

10 To paint the purple filler flowers, double load your no. 6 filbert with Dioxazine Purple and Titanium White and stroke on three one-stroke petals next to each other. Use a no. 4 filbert and Avocado to paint the base of each flower.

11 Use your no. 6 filbert brush and Violet Haze to paint backlights on the darkest areas of the leaves. Add water to Violet Haze and use your no. 6 filbert to stroke on one-stroke filler leaves around the design.

12 Repeat the design over the top and sides of the chest. When finished, varnish with several coats of J. W. etc. Right-Step Satin Varnish.

Gardener's Seed Company

When I was first introduced to decorative painting, what interested me most was the use of stroke flowers to accomplish a beautiful design quickly.

Painting stroke flowers does take a lot of practice. Even the most talented painter has to put in practice time when learning the strokes.

The more you paint, the looser your strokes should become. It is not necessary to fix every little imperfection. This is decorative art—not a screen print.

Preparation

1. Fill, sand and seal the wood. Base the entire box with Light Buttermilk.

2. When dry, tape off the sections for each seed packet. Base the bands around the seed packets with Mink Tan.

3. Transfer only minimal pattern lines for each flower.

Materials

DecoArt Americana Acrylic Paints

Titanium White DA1

Pineapple DA6

Cadmium Orange DA14

Lilac DA32

Olive Green DA56

Burnt Sienna DA63

Slate Grey DA68

Mink Tan DA92

Sapphire DA99

Dioxazine Purple DA101

Light Cinnamon DA114

Hauser Dark Green DA133

Antique Rose DA156

Light Buttermilk DA164

Napa Red DA165

Bittersweet Chocolate DA195

Violet Haze DA197

Primary Yellow DA201

Celery Green DA208

DecoArt Dazzling Metallics

Emperor's Gold DA148

Materials list continued on page 58.

Gardener's Seed Co.

SUNFLOWER

HOLLYHOCK

DAISY

RO

This pattern may be hand-traced or photocopied for personal use only. Reattach two halves and enlarge at 172% to return to full size.

Materials *continued*

Surface

This box has partitions inside and may be hung on the wall or displayed on a flat surface. It is available wholesale from Roland Nimmo, 9198 Bonita Drive, Cherry Valley, California 92223. Phone (909) 845-6527.

The box can also be purchased retail from The Tole Bridge, 1875 Norco Drive, Norco, California 91760. Phone (909) 272-6918.

Diane's Angel Series Brushes
• Diane's Angel Mist brush, ⅜-inch (1cm)

Loew-Cornell Brushes
• series 7050 10/0 liner
• series 7300 no. 2 flat
• series 7400 ⅜-inch (1cm) angle
• series 7500 no. 2, no. 4 and no. 6 filberts

Miscellaneous
• J.W. etc. Wood Filler
• fine sanding disc
• J.W. etc. First Step Wood Sealer
• masking tape
• tracing paper and pencil
• Chacopaper
• Kemper stylus
• DecoArt Gel Stain, Oak DS30
• J.W. etc. Right-Step Satin Varnish

Plants And Seeds

EST. 1887

ROSE

VIOLET

TULIP

GERANIUM

Diane Trierweiler ©

1 Use your no. 6 filbert brush to scumble in the background areas where the flowers will be on each seed packet. This is done with a dabbing motion using Celery Green and then Hauser Dark Green. This color should look faded. It is used to give the flowers something to sit on.

The Sunflowers

2 Use your Angel Mist brush to stipple in the centers of the sunflowers with Burnt Sienna. Stipple the center depression and around the outer edges of the centers using Bittersweet Chocolate.

3 Use your no. 6 filbert double loaded with Hauser Dark Green and Olive Green to stroke some leaves around the sunflowers. Keep the Hauser Dark Green side of the brush toward the center of the leaves.

4 Use your no. 6 filbert double loaded with Burnt Sienna and Primary Yellow to stroke on the petals. Press down on the brush and pull to the chisel edge, starting at the edge of your flower centers. You will have to go over your petals twice.

5 Use your no. 2 filbert double loaded with Pineapple and Primary Yellow to stroke smaller petals over the larger ones. Tint the edges of some petals with Cadmium Orange. Add Burnt Sienna lines on some petals using your liner brush. Use Pineapple to add a stippled highlight in the centers of the flowers. Tint the centers with a touch of Cadmium Orange on your angle brush.

6 Dot the seeds in with the tip of your liner brush using Hauser Dark Green plus Napa Red. The seeds should go all around the centers and should overlap onto the petals.

7 Use your 10/0 liner to make vein lines on the leaves with Olive Green. Use your liner brush and Olive Green to make tendrils around the flowers. Tint the edges of the leaves with Burnt Sienna.

8 With your no. 6 filbert, add Violet Haze in the darkest areas of the flowers and on the darkest areas of the leaves. This color should be carried throughout the design on all of the seed packets; it complements all of the shadow areas. The completed sunflower seed packet is shown on page 71.

The Hollyhocks

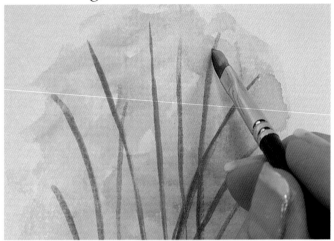

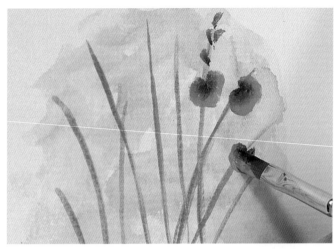

9 Scumble a dark area where the hollyhocks will sit using Celery Green and Hauser Dark Green. To create stems for the flowers, double load a no. 2 filbert with Celery Green and Hauser Dark Green and pull the brush on the chisel edge. Do not clean the brush when you have finished this step.

10 Use the brush from step nine to tap in small green blossoms at the end of the stems. To create the leaves, double load the no. 2 filbert with Celery Green and Hauser Dark Green. Press down on your brush and wiggle in a half circle to create the first half of a leaf.

11 Double load the no. 2 filbert with Celery Green and Hauser Dark Green again and stroke on the other half of your leaf.

12 Tint behind the leaves with a little Olive Green. Wash Hauser Dark Green under the stems to darken the ground area. When dry, tint the ground with Burnt Sienna. Use your no. 2 filbert double loaded with Sapphire and Titanium White. Wiggle your brush around in a half circle, leaving Sapphire on the outer edge of your flower.

13 Still using your no. 2 filbert, finish the other side of the flower. Start at the bottom of the stems with larger flowers and work your way to the top, gradually making the flowers smaller. Go over the petals twice for good coverage.

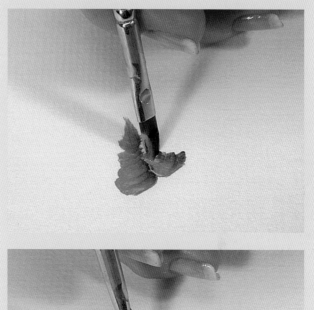

Hint
To create one-stroke leaves, wiggle your brush on the flat edge to form the base of the leaf and gradually pull up to the chisel edge to create the tip. Repeat on the other side of the leaf.

14 Use your liner brush and Primary Yellow to put tiny dots in the center of each flower. Also use your liner to stroke Sapphire lines radiating out from the centers. Tint the edges of the petals with Dioxazine Purple. Add a tint of Violet Haze here and there. See page 71 for the completed hollyhocks seed packet.

The Daisies

15 Stipple in the green background area as instructed for the sunflowers and hollyhocks. Use your no. 6 filbert and Primary Yellow to base the centers of the daisies. Use your no. 4 filbert and Slate Grey to stroke on the underpetals.

16 Double load your no. 4 filbert with Celery Green and Hauser Dark Green and stroke on one-stroke leaves.

17 Vary the size of your leaves—some should be double sided and some single sided. Use your liner brush to line in veins and tendrils with Hauser Dark Green. Tint some of the leaf edges with a float of Burnt Sienna. Tint some of the leaves with Olive Green.

18 Side load your angle brush with Burnt Sienna and shade the centers of the flowers. Highlight the centers of the flowers with a few dots of Pineapple on your liner.

19 Use your no. 6 filbert brush loaded with Titanium White to stroke over the grey petals. Let some of the Slate Grey show through. Use a mix of Hauser Dark Green plus Napa Red to pull a few lines from the center of your flower outward using your liner brush.

20 Dot seeds around the flower centers with your liner brush and the Hauser Dark Green/Napa Red mix from the previous step. Tint the edges of the petals with Dioxazine Purple. Tint the darkest areas of the flowers with Violet Haze. The completed daisy seed packet is shown on page 71.

The Roses

21 Scumble Celery Green and Hauser Dark Green into the background. Wash in the rose shapes with your no. 6 filbert brush and Antique Rose. See project seven for more detailed instructions on painting a rose.

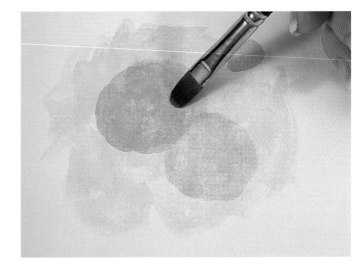

22 Side load your no. 6 filbert brush with Napa Red. Shade the cup and bowl of the rose.

23 Double load your ⅜-inch (1cm) angle brush with Antique Rose across three-fourths of the bristles and Light Buttermilk across one-fourth of the bristles. Blend the colors on your palette so that the Light Buttermilk becomes a pale rose color. Stroke in the back petals. Hold your brush away from the ferrule—this will give you less-structured flowers.

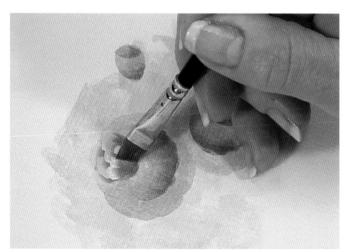

24 Finish the petals in the center back of the rosebud by dropping about ⅛ inch (0.3cm) for each row. Be sure that you alternate these layers to cover the previous separations in the petals.

25 Double load your ⅜-inch (1cm) angle brush with Antique Rose and Light Buttermilk and stroke one large petal on the front of the bud area.

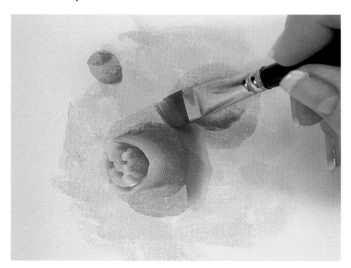

26 Double load your ⅜-inch (1cm) angle brush into Antique Rose and Light Buttermilk and stroke on the very bottom petal on the rose. This should be shaped like a slice of watermelon.

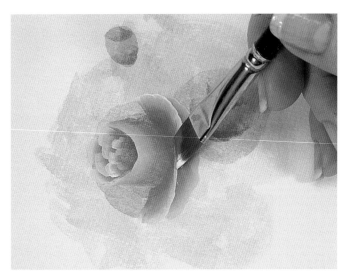

27 Double load your angle brush with Antique Rose and Light Buttermilk and begin stroking on side petals. Alternate from side to side.

28 The last two petals on the sides of the rose begin against the wall of the bud. Whenever you pull a stroke across the front of the bud, be sure you are on the chisel edge of your brush.

29 The last three petals on your rose are done with a double load of Antique Rose and Light Buttermilk. Press down lightly and immediately pull off to a chisel. These will represent just the edges of some petals and serve to fill in empty areas.

30 To give more depth to the centers of your roses, side load your angle brush into Napa Red and reshade. Paint the seeds in the center with Burnt Sienna on the end of the bristles of your liner brush.

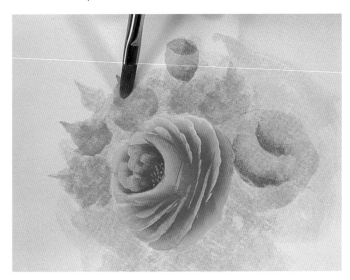

31 Add water to Celery Green. Using your no. 4 filbert brush, wash in your leaves.

32 Side load your no. 4 filbert brush into Hauser Dark Green. Shade the centers and edges of the leaves.

33 Use your liner brush and Hauser Dark Green to add veins and tendrils. Tint the edges of some of the leaves using Burnt Sienna. Wash a few highlights into the centers of the leaves using Olive Green. Add a few washes of Violet Haze in darkest areas for backlight. Tint a few of the rose petals with Dioxazine Purple. The completed rose seed packet is shown on page 71.

The Violets

34 Scumble in Celery Green and Hauser Dark Green behind the flowers. Use your no. 4 filbert double loaded with Olive Green and Hauser Dark Green to stroke on one-stroke leaves.

35 Paint the vein lines and tendrils with your liner brush using Hauser Dark Green. Tint the edges of the leaves with Dioxazine Purple.

36 Double load your no. 6 filbert with Lilac and Dioxazine Purple. Stroke on half of the large bottom petal first. The Dioxazine Purple should be on the outside edge.

37 Double load your no. 6 filbert with Lilac and Dioxazine Purple. Stroke on the second half of your bottom petal. The Dioxazine Purple should again be on the outside edge.

38 Double load your no. 4 filbert brush with Dioxazine Purple and Lilac. Stroke on two side petals, pressing down and pulling to a point to make comma strokes. The Dioxazine Purple edge of your brush should be facing the purple edge on the first large petal.

39 Double load your no. 4 filbert with Dioxazine Purple and Lilac and stroke two petals on top.

40 Tint some of the edges of the flowers with Napa Red. Use your liner brush and Primary Yellow to stroke tiny comma strokes into the centers of the flowers. Add one Napa Red dot in the center of each flower. Add a tiny Titanium White dot just above this one. Use your liner brush to pull small Dioxazine Purple lines onto the petals. Add Violet Haze into the darkest areas of the leaves and flowers. The completed violet seed packet is shown on page 71.

The Tulips

41 Scumble Celery Green and Hauser Dark Green behind the flowers. Double load the no. 4 filbert with Olive Green and Hauser Dark Green to make the leaves. Press down on your brush, starting from the ground area and pulling upward to a chisel. Overlap these leaves and make them different sizes. Use your liner brush and Hauser Dark Green to put in the flower stems.

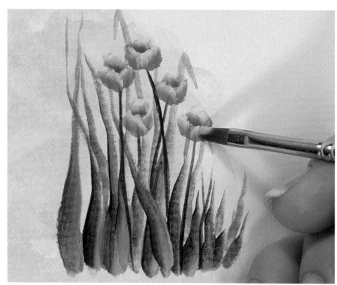

42 These tulips are shown in the distance, so they should be loose and impressionistic. Double load a no. 2 filbert with Antique Rose and Primary Yellow and stroke in the petals.

43 Use your no. 2 filbert to shade in the centers with Napa Red. Highlight here and there on each flower with Pineapple. Add Violet Haze in the darkest areas of the leaves and flowers. Darken the ground area with Hauser Dark Green. See page 71 for the completed tulip seed packet.

The Geraniums

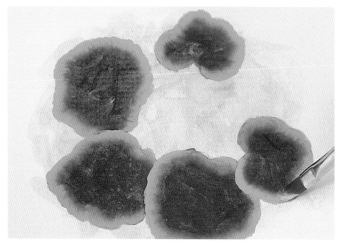

44 Scumble Celery Green and Hauser Dark Green where the flowers will be. Use your no. 6 filbert and Hauser Dark Green to base the leaves.

45 Load your no. 6 filbert with Olive Green and wiggle a highlight along the edges of the leaves.

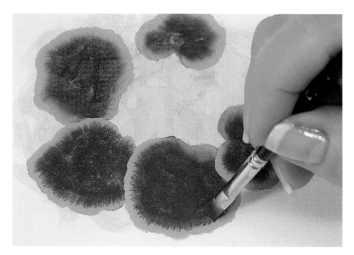

46 Use Napa Red plus water and your no. 2 flat to create a red band around the inner edges of the leaves. Tap lightly on the chisel edge of the brush to do this.

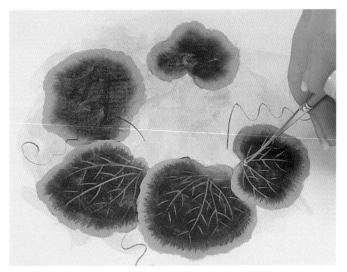

47 Use your liner brush and Olive Green to paint veins on the leaves. Use your liner brush and Hauser Dark Green to paint tendrils.

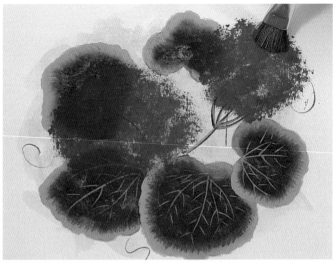

48 Use your Angel Mist brush to stipple Napa Red circles for the flowers. Use your liner brush to add a Hauser Dark Green stem for the side-view flower.

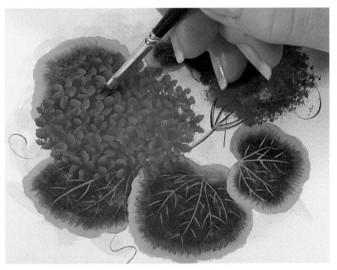

49 Double load your no. 2 filbert with Napa Red and Antique Rose. Begin to stroke on one-stroke flowers over the entire stippled area. Some flowers should have two petals and others should have three or five petals.

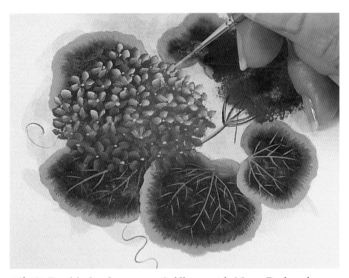

50 Double load your no. 2 filbert with Napa Red and Antique Rose. Blend these colors on your palette and add just a little Titanium White to the Antique Rose edge. Add highlights here and there on some of the petals. Use your liner brush bristles and Primary Yellow to put in the centers of the flowers.

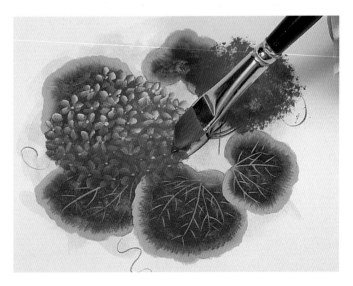

51 Use your angle brush and Napa Red to shade the bottom of each flower. Add Violet Haze to the darkest areas of the flowers and leaves. The completed geranium seed packet is shown on the next page.

SUNFLOWER

HOLLYHOCK

DAISY

ROSE

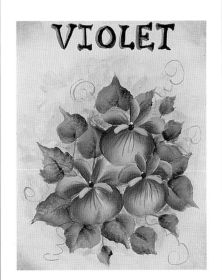

VIOLET

TULIP

GERANIUM

52 Use your liner brush and Hauser Dark Green to put lettering on the box. Line each letter on the left side with Emperor's Gold. Shade between seed packets with your angle brush and Light Cinnamon. Stain the entire box with Oak Gel Stain. Use a soft rag to wipe out almost all of the stain in the centers of each seed packet. Varnish with at least two coats of J. W. etc. Right-Step Satin Varnish.

The Wicker Rocker

If you like the Victorian era and all things Victorian, you probably have an affinity for things made from wicker. The Victorians used wicker furniture throughout their homes and gardens. The wicker pieces were painted in a variety of colors and had many intricate designs.

Wicker is not a difficult texture to paint; it just takes a little time to get the layered dimensional weave that makes it look realistic.

Picture yourself rocking in this chair, reading a book and relaxing.

If you like to paint wicker as much as I do, try painting it in other colors besides white.

Preparation

1. Fill, sand and seal the wood. The cabinet itself is based with your large glazing brush and Delta Ceramcoat Tide Pool Blue. Do not paint the door.

2. Transfer the pattern for the floor line onto the door.

3. Base everything above the floor line with Light Buttermilk. Base the floor with Toffee on your flat brush.

4. Transfer the pattern for the window. Tape off the area where the window will be.

Materials

DecoArt Americana Acrylic Paints

Titanium White DA1	Cadmium Yellow DA10	Dusty Rose DA25	Olive Green DA56	Toffee DA59	Slate Grey DA68
Evergreen DA82	Sapphire DA99	Dioxazine Purple DA101	Antique Maroon DA160	Graphite DA161	Antique Mauve DA162
Light Buttermilk DA164	French Mauve DA186	Winter Blue DA190	Violet Haze DA197	Antique Maroon + Slate Grey mix	

Delta Ceramcoat

Tide Pool Blue 02465

Materials list continued on page 75.

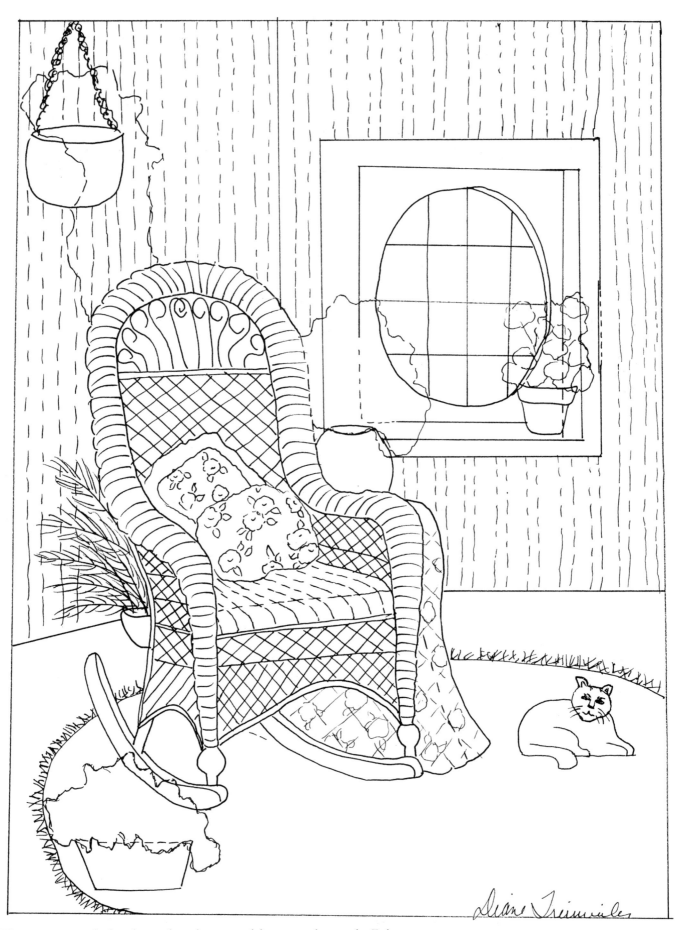

This pattern may be hand-traced or photocopied for personal use only. Enlarge at
125% to return to full size.

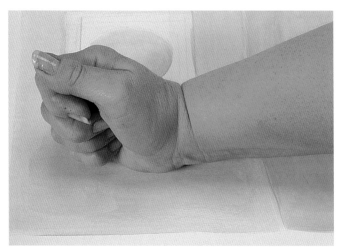

1 Base the wall with a mix of half Faux Glazing Medium and half Winter Blue. The glaze will help keep the paint workable long enough to texture it. While the wall is still wet, press the edge of your fist over the entire wall area, creating a subtle texture.

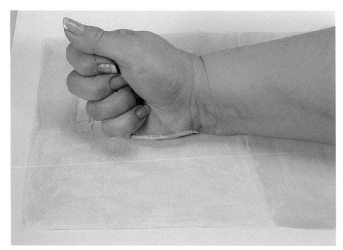

2 Now glaze over the wall with a mix of half Titanium White and half Faux Glazing Medium. Press the edge of your fist over the entire wall area again. Remove the tape from the window area and transfer the pattern for the window and rug.

3 Add water to Evergreen and use your no. 2 filbert to scumble a few leaves where the bush shows outside the window. Repeat with Olive Green. Add loose branch lines with a mix of Slate Grey and Antique Maroon, using your liner brush. Float an Evergreen shadow over the leaves on the left side of the window opening. Repeat on the right side of the window with Winter Blue.

Materials continued

Surface
This small cupboard may be purchased from Stan Brown Arts and Crafts, 13435 N. E. Whitaker Way, Portland, Oregon 97230. Phone (800) 547-5531.

Loew-Cornell Brushes
- series 798 ¾-inch (1.9cm) glazing brush
- series 7050 10/0 liner
- series 7300 no. 6 flat
- series 7400 ½-inch (1.3cm) angle
- series 7500 no. 2 filbert

Diane's Angel Series Brushes
- Diane's Angel Mist brush, ⅜-inch (1cm)

Miscellaneous
- J.W. etc. Wood Filler
- fine sanding disc
- J.W. etc. First Step Wood Sealer
- tracing paper and pencil
- Chacopaper
- Kemper stylus
- masking tape
- DecoArt Faux Glazing Medium DS18
- J.W. etc. Right-Step Satin Varnish

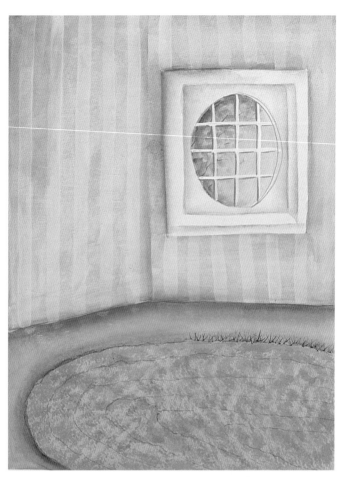

4 Use your liner brush and Titanium White to line in the windowpanes. Line on the bottom and left sides of the white lines with Slate Grey. Tint the window frame with Violet Haze. Add water to Titanium White and use your flat brush to paint the wallpaper stripes on the wall. Use your angle brush to shade the window frame and wall with Slate Grey. Tint the shadow areas of the wall with Violet Haze. Use your angle brush to shade next to the wall on the floor with Antique Maroon. Add water to Antique Maroon and use your Angel Mist brush to lightly stipple a softly textured rug on the floor. Use your liner brush and Antique Maroon to line in fringe and detail lines on the rug.

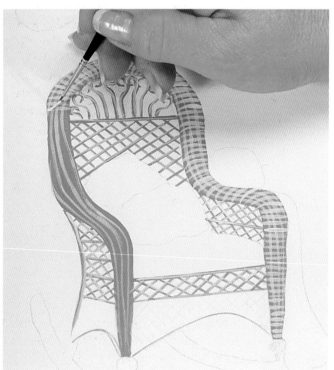

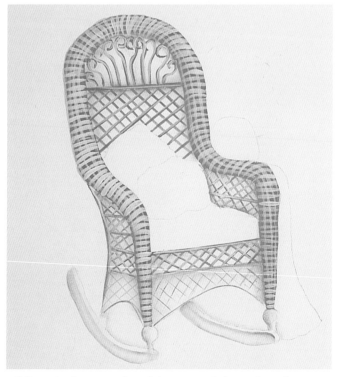

5 When the wall is dry, transfer the remaining pattern lines. Base the arms and back of the rocker with a mix of Slate Grey and a small amount of Antique Maroon. Use your liner brush to base the open latticework areas with this mix. Paint the first layer of weave with your liner brush and Light Buttermilk.

6 Base the bottom edge of the seat and the rockers themselves with Titanium White. Use your angle brush to put your first shading on the rocking chair with Slate Grey.

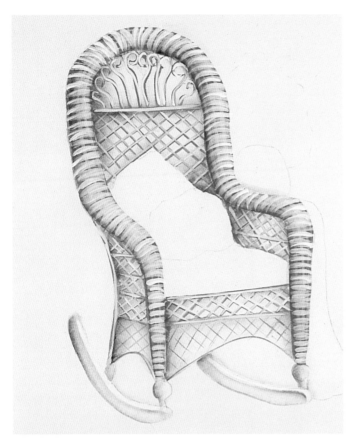

7 Use your liner brush and Titanium White to add the second layer of weave on the rocker. Use your angle brush to shade the rocker again using Graphite. With Cadmium Yellow tint the areas where the sun is hitting the chair.

8 Base the rocker cushion and pillow with Light Buttermilk. Base the tablecloth with Titanium White. Add water to Winter Blue and use your liner brush to make stripes on the chair cushion. Paint the roses on the pillows and tablecloth very loosely. Using your filbert brush and Antique Mauve plus water, wash in some small circles for the roses. Add a little Antique Maroon to the centers. Add water to Evergreen and use your filbert brush to wash in a few leaves. Tap in a little Winter Blue piping around the square pillow using your liner brush. Repeat around the round pillow using French Mauve.

9 Add water to Sapphire and use your liner brush to paint in crosshatch lines on the tablecloth. Use your angle brush and Slate Grey to shade the pillows, chair cushion and tablecloth. Use your angle brush and Antique Maroon to shade under everything sitting on the rug. Use your angle brush and Graphite to add a second shade to the deepest corners around and on the tablecloth, pillows and chair cushion. Tint the darkest shadow areas with Violet Haze. Add water to Violet Haze and tap in tiny filler flowers around the roses.

10 Base the flowerpot in the window with Dusty Rose on a flat brush. Shade the pot with Antique Maroon and highlight it with Titanium White. Base the flowerpot on the rug with a mix of Slate Grey and Sapphire. Highlight the pot with a float of Light Buttermilk. Base the flowerpot on the table with Titanium White. Use Sapphire on your liner brush to squiggle in pattern lines. Shade with a float of Slate Grey. Base the hanging plant in the upper left corner with Dusty Rose. Shade with Antique Maroon. Line the rope in with Dusty Rose and then with Antique Maroon while it is still wet. Base the flowerpot behind the rocker with Titanium White and shade with Graphite. Double load your no. 2 filbert with Olive Green and Evergreen. Wiggle the brush in circles to create geranium leaves in the pot on the window. Use your liner brush and Evergreen to line in the fern. While the Evergreen is still wet, line over the fern leaves with Olive Green. Double load your no. 2 filbert with Evergreen and Olive Green and stroke one-stroke leaves in the remaining flowerpots.

11 Paint round flowers in the pot on the window shelf with your no. 2 filbert and a double load of Antique Mauve and Titanium White, tapping with the chisel edge of your brush. Paint the flowers in the pot on the rug with a double load of Dioxazine Purple and Titanium White. They are tiny one-stroke flowers. Paint the flowers in the pot on the table with double loads of Antique Mauve and Titanium White, Sapphire and Titanium White, and Violet Haze and Titanium White. They are also tiny one-stroke flowers. Use Sapphire to dab in tiny flowers coming out of the hanging flowerpot. Add Violet Haze to the shadow areas of all the flowerpots and in the darkest areas of the flowers.

12 Use your Angel Mist brush to drybrush Titanium White streaks through the windowpanes. Carry these streaks across the room, touching down on the rocker. Lightly touch into the windowpanes with paint to create reflections. Basecoat the cat with Slate Grey. Use your liner brush and Titanium White to paint the cat's fur. Be sure to leave some of the Slate Grey underpaint showing through. Wash a little Dusty Rose into the ears and onto the nose and shade with Antique Maroon. Line the whiskers with Slate Grey. Fill in the eyes with Antique Maroon, using your liner brush. Tint the shadow areas on the cat with Violet Haze. Highlight with more Titanium White linework.

Yellow Roses and Lilacs

Almost everyone loves roses, yet many people find them difficult to paint. I spent many hours in pursuit of the elusive rose until I finally devised a basic method for painting one. Take some time to practice these steps and don't give up. Once you have the basic form and values in mind, you can branch out to create your own style of rose.

There are so many uses for this wonderful flower!

Preparation

1. Fill, sand and seal the wood. Use your large glazing brush to base the surface with Light Buttermilk.

2. Base the bottom of the box with Evergreen.

3. Transfer minimal pattern lines.

Materials

DecoArt Americana Acrylic Paints

Titanium White DA1

Pineapple DA6

Antique Gold DA9

Cadmium Red DA15

Burnt Sienna DA63

Evergreen DA82

Dioxazine Purple DA101

Light Avocado DA106

Viridian Green DA108

Yellow Green DA134

Red Violet DA140

Light Buttermilk DA164

Violet Haze DA197

Surface

This box is called a mushroom box. It comes in various sizes and can be purchased from Valhalla Designs, 343 Twin Pines Drive, Glendale, Oregon 97442. Phone (541) 832-3260.

Diane's Angel Series Brushes

- Diane's Angel Wing brushes, ½-inch (1.3cm) and ⅜-inch (1cm)

Loew-Cornell Brushes

- series 275 ½-inch (1.3cm) mop
- series 798 ¾-inch (1.9cm) glazing brush
- series 7050 10/0 liner
- series 7400 ½-inch (1.3cm) and ⅝-inch (1.6cm) angles
- series 7500 no. 2 and no. 10 filberts

Miscellaneous

- J.W. etc. Wood Filler
- fine sanding disc

- J.W. etc. First Step Wood Sealer
- tracing paper and pencil
- Chacopaper
- Kemper stylus
- gold leaf adhesive and old brush
- variegated gold leaf
- DecoArt Gel Stain, Oak DS30
- DecoArt Matte Spray
- J.W. etc. Right-Step Satin Varnish

This pattern may be hand-traced or photocopied for personal use only. Enlarge at 133% to return to full size.

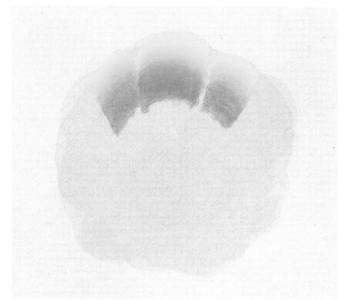

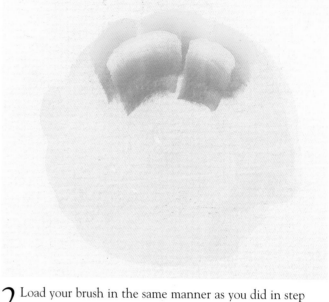

1 Wash in a circle for the rose using Antique Gold and a lot of water; this is done just for placement. Double load your angle brush with Antique Gold and Pineapple. The darker value (Antique Gold) should cover three-fourths of the brush and the lighter value (Pineapple) should cover only one-fourth of the brush. Stroke three large petals across the back of the rose. This first layer of petals is darkest in value. This is achieved by brushing the Pineapple edge of your brush slightly into Antique Gold to darken it.

2 Load your brush in the same manner as you did in step one, but allow the Pineapple edge of the stroke to be lighter in value. Add the next layer of petals inside the rose, overlapping the first layer.

Hint
To determine the size of the angle brush you should use when painting a rose, keep this guideline in mind: You should be able to fit three widths of the brush you are using inside the width of the rose.

Hint
Visually divide your rose into thirds horizontally and vertically. The bud of the rose should fall in the center section.

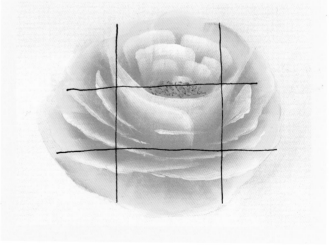

3 Add the last layer of bud petals. These petals are smaller than the previous layers. Darken the center of the rose with a float of Antique Gold on your angle brush.

4 Load your angle brush with Antique Gold and Pineapple, tipping the Pineapple edge into Antique Gold to achieve the darkest-value light you used in step one. With this color, add one large petal across the front of your bud, Pineapple edge up. Add another petal at the base of the bud, with the Antique Gold edge touching the bottom of the bud and the Pineapple side down. This petal should resemble a slice of watermelon. Do not cover the bottom of the bud or pull your stroke any higher than the bud area.

5 Double load your angle brush with Antique Gold and Pineapple; this should be a lighter value than in step four. Drop below the petal you painted across the front of the bud and stroke one more petal across the front, stopping in the middle of the rose and pulling down on your chisel. Load your brush again and begin to alternate side petals on the rose. Press your bristles down to start the petal and gradually pull up to the chisel edge to finish. Pull your stroke past the center of the rose horizontally. Place the next side petal stroke just above this one.

6 Continue in the same manner as in step five and add two more side petals above the previous petals.

7 Start the last set of side petals against the side of the bud. Press down to begin and pull up to the chisel edge to finish. These petals do not necessarily need to be pulled across the center. They may stop short. Be sure not to cover up your bud area as you pull the side strokes on.

8 Double load your angle brush with Antique Gold and Pineapple and very lightly and quickly touch down and pull up for the three filler strokes in the center of the rose, just above the last layer of side petals. When all the petals are dry, glaze over the entire rose with Yellow Green.

9 When the glaze is dry, side load your angle brush with Light Buttermilk and highlight a few of the petal edges. Side load your angle brush with Cadmium Red and tint a few of the edges of the rose petals for warmth. Dot in the stamen with Burnt Sienna and Emperor's Gold.

10 Load your liner brush with water and Burnt Sienna to line loose twigs behind your roses.

11 Use your no. 10 filbert and Light Avocado to wash in leaf shapes very loosely. This should be a very transparent color.

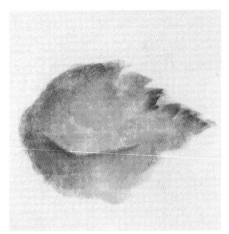

12 Use your ½-inch (1.3cm) angle to shade each leaf with Evergreen.

13 Tint each leaf with small amounts of Viridian Green and Yellow Green. This is done with your no. 10 filbert brush and a lot of water.

14 Use your no. 10 filbert brush and Burnt Sienna to float a "burn" on the edges of each leaf. This color should be placed in different areas on each leaf so that all the leaves don't look the same.

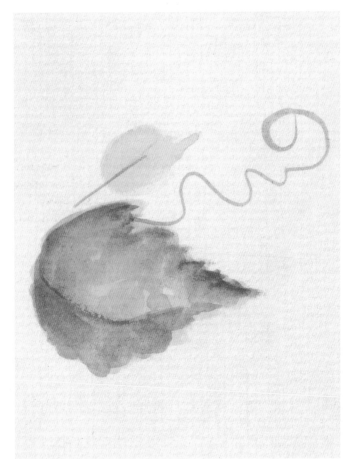

15 Use your liner brush and a mix of Burnt Sienna plus Evergreen to line in tendrils. Tint the leaves with Red Violet. Add water to Violet Haze and wash in faded background leaves with your no. 10 filbert.

16 Use your liner brush and Evergreen to add vein lines to the leaves.

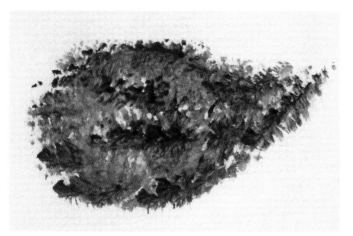

17 Use your Angel Wing brush to stipple the lilac shapes with Dioxazine Purple.

18 Use your Angel Wing brush to stipple in Red Violet over the purple.

19 Double load your no. 2 filbert with Titanium White and Dioxazine Purple. Make tiny one-stroke petals over the lilac shapes. Vary the florets from two or three to five petals.

20 Dot Yellow Green in the centers of the florets with your liner. Use your angle brush to shade the bottoms of the lilacs with Red Violet.

21 To complete the design, add water to Light Avocado and wash around the entire design. Use your no. 2 filbert and Titanium White to stroke on small filler flowers next to the roses and in various spots throughout the design. Varnish with at least two coats of J.W. etc. Right-Step Satin Varnish.

22 Spatter the design area with Emperor's Gold and an Angel Wing brush or toothbrush and palette knife. See page 13 for instructions.

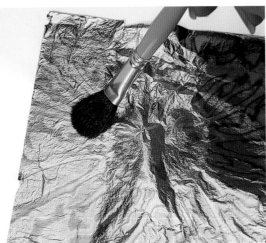

23 Use an old brush to paint gold leaf adhesive on the base of the box. Let dry for about half an hour. Place small pieces of gold leaf over the adhesive. Let some of the green paint show here and there. Gold leaf can become discolored over time due to oxidization, as mine has. I don't mind this, as it adds to the aged appearance of the piece.

24 Next, brush off the unglued pieces. Burnish the leaf with a mop brush.

25 Spray the gold leaf with matte spray. Let dry, then antique the leafing with Oak Gel Stain. Varnish again with J.W. etc. Right-Step Satin Varnish.

Autumn at the Farm

*A*lthough it's nice to paint a variety of colorful summer flowers around an old farmhouse, I've chosen to present you with a new challenge in this piece. This project will teach you how make fall paintings interesting using backlight mixes and warm fall colors.

This scene reminds me of fall in Wisconsin, where I was born.

Preparation

There is no need to seal this rusted metal piece. Simply transfer the pattern for the outer oval, horizon line and house.

Materials

DecoArt Americana Acrylic Paints

Titanium White DA1	Antique Gold DA9	Georgia Clay DA17	Sea Aqua DA46	Avocado DA52	Mocha DA60
Slate Grey DA68	Dove Grey DA69	Dioxazine Purple DA101	Hauser Light Green DA131	Burnt Sienna DA63	Burnt Umber DA64
Prussian Blue DA138	Graphite DA161	Payne's Grey DA167	Marigold DA194	Bittersweet Chocolate DA195	Violet Haze DA197

Soft Peach DA216

DecoArt Dazzling Metallics

Emperor's Gold DA148

Materials list continued on page 94.

This pattern may be hand-traced or photocopied for personal use only. Reattach
two halves and enlarge at 118% to return to full size.

1 The sky will need more than one layer of color; apply the sky colors wet-on-wet. Moisten the sky area with Faux Glazing Medium. Use your ½-inch (1.3cm) filbert to blend Prussian Blue and Titanium White into the sky. Paint one small area at a time, then use your mop brush to soften the colors. Blend Soft Peach into the lightest areas.

2 After you have completed the sky area and none of the underneath metal is showing, tint it with washes of Dioxazine Purple and Georgia Clay. Your sky should be lightest at the horizon line.

Materials continued

Surface

This piece comes in a set of two sizes—one fits into the other. You may paint another design on the smaller of the two sizes. These metal pieces may be purchased from The Tole Bridge, 1875 Norco Drive, Norco, California 91760. Phone (909) 272-6918.

Diane's Angel Series Brushes

- Diane's Angel Mist brush, ⅜-inch (1cm)
- Diane's Angel Wing brush, ⅜-inch (1cm)

Loew-Cornell Brushes

- series 275 ½-inch (1.3cm) mop
- series 7050 10/0 liner
- series 7300 no. 6 flat
- series 7400 ½-inch (1.3cm) angle
- series 7500 no. 4 and ½-inch (1.3cm) filberts

Miscellaneous

- DecoArt Faux Glazing Medium DS18
- tracing paper and pencil
- Chacopaper
- Kemper stylus
- J.W. etc. Right-Step Satin Varnish

3 Use your angle brush to float in Soft Peach clouds.

4 Make a mixture of half Payne's Grey and half Dioxazine Purple. Add water to this mix and use your Angel Mist brush to stipple the background trees in.

5 Use your liner brush and Mocha to paint the tree trunks. While the Mocha is still wet, use Bittersweet Chocolate to add bark and shadows.

6 Use your Angel Mist brush to stipple darker pockets of leaves on the trees using Payne's Grey.

7 Use your Angel Mist brush to start stippling foliage onto the trees using Antique Gold and then Georgia Clay.

8 Use your Angel Mist brush to stipple a second layer of leaves onto the trees with Avocado and Sea Aqua.

9 Stipple a little Violet Haze into the darkest areas to create the backlights.

10 Base the walls of the house with Dove Grey and your no. 6 flat brush. Base the roof with Burnt Sienna. Use your liner brush to paint siding lines on the walls of the house with Slate Grey. Fill in the windows and doors with Graphite.

11 Use your liner brush and Titanium White to add highlight siding lines and trim on the house. Use Burnt Sienna to add a few more siding lines on the walls. Use your angle brush to shade the walls of the house with Slate Grey. Shade again in the darker areas with Graphite.

12 Use your liner brush to line in shingles on the roof. Use Bittersweet Chocolate on the dark side of the roof and Mocha on the light side. Mix Mocha and Georgia Clay for the very lightest shingles.

13 Use your angle brush and Bittersweet Chocolate to shade the roof. Shade around the windows with Graphite. Use your liner brush and Titanium White to line in the windowpanes and gingerbread on the house.

14 Wash transparent curtains in the windows with Titanium White. Use Violet Haze to tint the shadow side of the house and roof. Use your liner brush and Graphite to line in the weather vane on the roof.

15 Stipple Payne's Grey and Dioxazine Purple in the flower beds. Then stipple flowers in with Georgia Clay, Avocado, Marigold, Sea Aqua and Antique Gold.

16 Base the walls of the barn with the no. 6 flat brush and Georgia Clay. While the paint is still wet, line in some Burnt Umber to create board lines on the walls.

17 Highlight the light side of the walls with the angle brush and Antique Gold brush mixed with Georgia Clay. Base the windows and doors with Burnt Umber.

18 Use your angle brush to shade the barn walls with Burnt Umber, then again with Graphite. Highlight the window and door openings with a float of Titanium White. Base the roof with Burnt Umber. Highlight the roof with a float of Mocha. Use your liner brush and Burnt Umber to line in shingles. Line in some Mocha highlights along the roof edges.

19 Shade the roof with your angle brush and Graphite. Add Violet Haze in the darkest areas of the roof and walls.

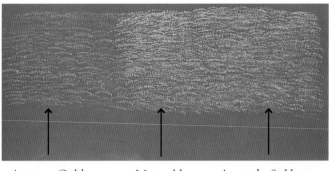

Antique Gold   Marigold   Avocado & Hauser
Light Green

20 Paint the grass with your Angel Wing brush. Add water to Antique Gold and jab and pull down with your brush over the grass area. Let the rust color of the surface show through a little. Repeat in the lightest areas with Marigold. Let dry and add more grass using Avocado and then Hauser Light Green—this is a fall scene, so do not add too much green.

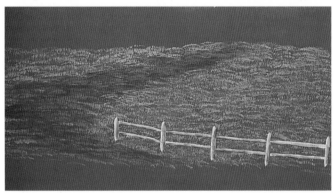

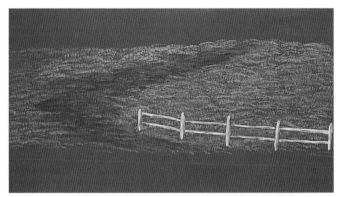

21 Use your liner brush and Dove Grey to paint in the fence. Add water to Burnt Umber and wash in a path in front of the barn and house.

22 Use your liner brush and Burnt Umber to line the right side and bottom of the fence. Highlight the left side and top of each board with a slash of Sea Aqua. Touch a little Violet Haze into the shadow areas with your liner brush.

23 Use your no. 4 filbert brush to base the rocks. Do this in a wet-on-wet method with Mocha and Graphite. Shade with Graphite and then with Payne's Grey.

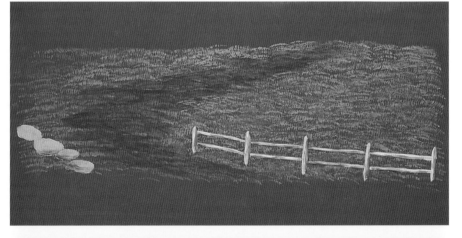

24 Float Violet Haze in the darkest areas on the rocks with your angle brush.

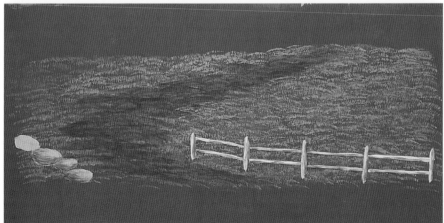

25 To complete the painting, use your liner brush to line in some grass around the rocks with Avocado, Hauser Light Green and Sea Aqua. Stipple in some tiny flowers near the rocks with your Angel Mist brush. First use Prussian Blue and Titanium White, then Georgia Clay and Antique Gold. Shade along the horizon line with your angle brush and Payne's Grey and Bittersweet Chocolate. Paint the trees behind the barn in the same way as the ones in the far distance. Stipple around the base of the barn with your Angel Mist brush and Payne's Grey and Dioxazine Purple. Add a little bit of color around your barn with stipples of Avocado, Georgia Clay, Antique Gold and Sea Aqua. Base the oval bands on each side of the scene with Avocado. Line both sides of the bands with Emperor's Gold. When dry, wash over the bands with Burnt Umber to tone them down. Varnish the entire tin with at least two coats of J. W. etc. Right-Step Satin Varnish.

Breakfast by the Sea

There are many old Victorian homes like this along the California coast and on Puget Sound in Washington.

With this design, I wanted to capture that wonderful feeling of looking out to the ocean from the lawn of an old home that is now a bed-and-breakfast.

This project presents a good opportunity to change your sky colors and landline to create variety in your work.

This tray can be a functional piece; adding a piece of glass over the painting will help protect it. Display it on the wall or on a shelf when not in use. You may choose to paint this design on a piece of furniture instead.

Materials

DecoArt Americana Acrylic Paints

Titanium White DA1	Moon Yellow DA7	Cadmium Yellow DA10
Williamsburg Blue DA40	Sea Aqua DA46	Olive Green DA56
Jade Green DA57	Burnt Sienna DA63	Dark Chocolate DA65
Evergreen DA82	Neutral Grey DA95	Sapphire DA99
Rookwood Red DA97	Dioxazine Purple DA101	Hauser Dark Green DA133
Graphite DA161	Light Buttermilk DA164	Violet Haze DA197
Peony Pink DA215	Soft Peach DA216	

Ceramichrome Softees

Irish Cream SS21
(or mix DecoArt Americana Titanium White DA1 + Yellow Green DA134)

Materials list continued on page 104.

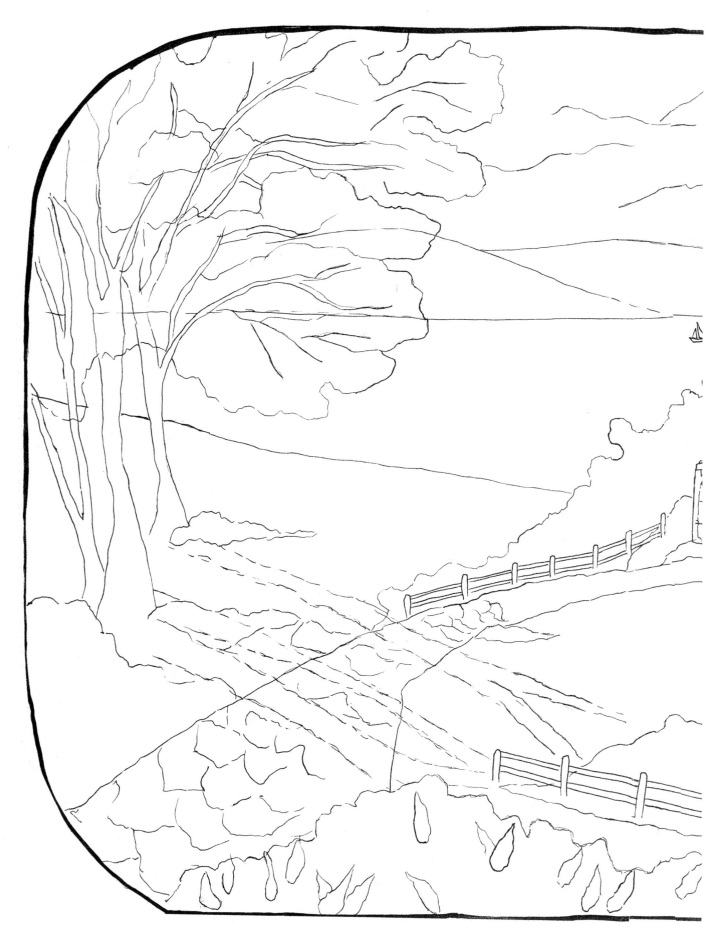

This pattern may be hand-traced or photocopied for personal use only. Reattach
two halves and enlarge at 147% to return to full size.

Preparation

1. Mask off the inside base of the tray with newspaper and masking tape. Spray the wicker areas with flat white spray paint.

2. When the spray paint is dry, remove the newspaper and tape. Fill and sand the tray base, then seal it with J.W. etc. White Lightning plus a little Light Buttermilk.

3. When working on a landscape, I usually use a half-and-half mix of paint and water to wash in all of the elements for placement and then come back later with full-strength paint. Transfer minimal pattern lines and base the areas as follows: the sky with Soft Peach; the background hills with a mix of half Neutral Grey and half Violet Haze; the water with Williamsburg Blue and the grass with Jade Green.

Materials continued

Surface

The wicker on this tray is handcrafted and of very good quality. You may purchase this and many other trays from Hofcraft, 1730-B Air Park Drive, Grand Haven, Michigan 49417. Phone (616) 847-8989.

Diane's Angel Series Brushes

- Diane's Angel Mist brush, ⅜-inch (1cm)
- Diane's Angel Wing brush, ⅜-inch (1cm)

Loew-Cornell Brushes

- series 275 ½-inch (1.3cm) mop
- series 7050 10/0 liner
- series 7300 no. 2, no. 8 and no. 12 flats
- series 7400 ½-inch (1.3cm) angle
- series 7500 ½-inch (1.3cm) and no. 6 filberts

Miscellaneous

- masking tape
- old newspaper
- flat white spray paint (any inexpensive brand)
- J.W. etc. Wood Filler
- fine sanding disc
- J. W. etc. White Lightning
- tracing paper and pencil
- Chacopaper
- Kemper stylus
- J. W. etc. Right-Step Satin Varnish

1 Using your ½-inch (1.3cm) filbert, dampen a small area of the sky with Soft Peach plus a little water. While the area is still wet, scumble in Moon Yellow and Peony Pink. Mop the area softly. Cover the entire sky using this wet-on-wet method, working one small area at a time.

2 When the sky is dry, wash in Williamsburg Blue here and there and then mop to soften. When this is dry, use your filbert brush and Light Buttermilk to float in clouds. Soften the clouds with your mop brush before they dry.

3 Tint the clouds with washes of Peony Pink, Violet Haze and Sea Aqua. Apply these colors separately to prevent muddying.

4 Use your no. 12 flat brush to add some pockets of light color here and there on the hills. Do this with Soft Peach, Moon Yellow and Peony Pink.

5 Use your no. 12 flat brush to add Williamsburg Blue shadows here and there on the hills. Add Titanium White to Violet Haze and brush on highlights in a few areas. Work wet-on-wet with these colors until you are satisfied with the results. The hills are quite far in the distance and should not stand out. Make sure they remain faded and obscure.

6 Use the chisel edge of your no. 8 flat brush to add highlights to the water with Moon Yellow, Peony Pink and Soft Peach.

7 Use Williamsburg Blue to streak dark shadows onto the water. Use the chisel edge of your no. 8 flat brush. Rehighlight through the center area of the water with Titanium White.

8 Tint the water with washes of Sea Aqua and Sapphire.

9 Use your filbert brush to wash some shadows in the grass with Hauser Dark Green.

10 Deepen the grass shadow areas with a wash of Violet Haze.

11 Wash over the lightest areas with Olive Green. Mix Olive Green plus Titanium White and a little water. To create small blades of grass on the lawn, tap and pull down on your Angel Wing brush. Use your Angel Wing brush and Irish Cream on the highest points of the hills for your last highlight. Tint the lawn with Peony Pink in the light areas and Sea Aqua in the shadow areas.

12 Base the roof of the house with a solid coat of Neutral Grey. Wash in the walls with Moon Yellow. Base the chimney and foundation with a mix of half Burnt Sienna and half Soft Peach. Wash inside of the windows with Williamsburg Blue.

13 Base the peaks on the front face of the house with Titanium White. Use your liner brush to line in the siding with Neutral Grey. Base all the trim on the house with your liner brush and Titanium White. Shade the walls with your angle brush and Neutral Grey.

14 Side load your no. 12 flat brush with Graphite and touch down on the chisel edge to create shingles on the roof. Shade the roof with your angle brush and Graphite.

15 Highlight the roof with your angle brush and Soft Peach. Use your liner brush to add slashes of Light Buttermilk in the highlight areas. Shade one edge of each window with a float of Williamsburg Blue.

16 Use your liner brush to line in the windowpanes with Titanium White. Add water to various bright colors on your palette and wash in the stained glass panels. Float Violet Haze over all the dark areas on the walls and roof of your house.

17 Add water to Rookwood Red and use your liner brush to place in small bricks on the foundation and chimney. Repeat here and there with Neutral Grey. Shade the steps with Neutral Grey.

18 Shade the chimney with Burnt Sienna using your angle brush. Highlight the chimney with a float of Soft Peach. Tint here and there using Violet Haze to create backlights.

19 Tint the steps with Violet Haze. Paint the door handle with Graphite and your liner brush. The completed house is shown below. Use your liner brush and Dark Chocolate to line in branches for the trees behind the house. Use your Angel Mist brush to stipple in foliage on the trees with Violet Haze, Hauser Dark Green, Jade Green, Olive Green and Irish Cream. When dry, float Hauser Dark Green next to the house to add shadows to the trees. Use your Angel Mist brush to stipple Hauser Dark Green and Olive Green into the flower beds. The flowers are stippled wet-on-wet with various colors from your palette, such as Dioxazine Purple and Titanium White, Peony Pink and Titanium White, Sapphire and Titanium White, Moon Yellow and Titanium White and Sea Aqua and Titanium White. Dab in a little Violet Haze in the darkest areas of the trees and flower beds for backlights.

The completed flowers and foliage.

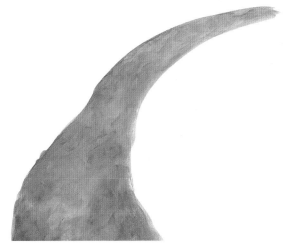

20 Base the path with a wash of Neutral Grey.

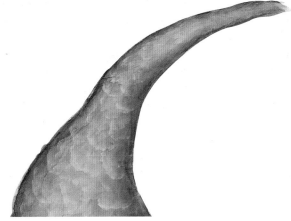

21 Working wet-on-wet with your no. 6 filbert brush, scumble Neutral Grey and Light Buttermilk onto the path. Highlight through the center of the path with Soft Peach. Shade along the sides of the path with a float of Graphite on your angle brush.

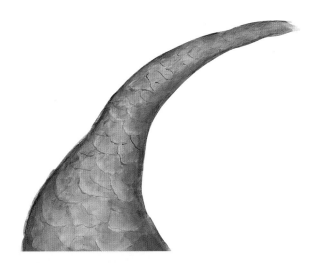

22 Use your liner brush and Graphite to squiggle in some grout lines. Tint the shadow areas of the path using Violet Haze.

23 Base the sailboat with Neutral Grey. Base the sails with Titanium White. Shade the sails with a little Neutral Grey. Use your liner brush and Titanium White to line under the boat to create small waves.

24 Base the larger tree trunks with Neutral Grey plus Light Buttermilk. Use your filbert brush and Titanium White to highlight the tree trunks.

25 Shade the trunks with a float of Dark Chocolate. Side load your no. 6 filbert brush and slide on the chisel edge to create the bark on the trunks Shade the shadow areas with a float of Violet Haze. Paint the foliage on the trees in the same way as you did the trees behind the house.

26 To create shadows cast on the ground, add water to Neutral Grey and wash over the grass and path, following the shapes of the trees.

27 To finish the design, use your liner brush and Dark Chocolate to line in some branches where your forefront bushes will be. Stipple in foliage using Hauser Dark Green, Jade Green and Olive Green. Stipple the flowers wet-on-wet with your Angel Mist brush and Peony Pink and Titanium White, Dioxazine Purple and Titanium White, Sea Aqua and Titanium White, Moon Yellow and Titanium White and Sapphire and Titanium White. The flowers in the forefront of the scene are a little more detailed than those around the house. Paint these as instructed for the forefront flowers in project ten on page 125. Use various greens from your palette and your liner brush to line in small grasses along the edges of the path. Paint the fence following the step-by-

step pictures for project eight, page 98. Use your no. 2 flat to base the fence with Titanium White. Use your liner brush and Neutral Grey to add shadows to the fence. Use your liner brush and Violet Haze to add some backlight to the shadow sides of the fence. With Neutral Grey create cast shadows coming off the fence. Make sure you have shaded around all of the flower beds with Hauser Dark Green and a little Violet Haze. If there is too much flower color in your flower beds, restipple a little more green over the flowers. Check that all shadow areas have a little Violet Haze in them to create backlights. Varnish the base of the tray with at least two coats of J.W. etc. Right-Step Satin Varnish.

The Dover Cottage

A few years ago my husband and I took a trip to Europe and spent time in England. I've never forgotten the Tudor cottages in the countryside near London. The locals have preserved the cottages, and the gardens around them are very well kept and beautiful.

Some of the stone walls bordering the cottages have been there since the time of the Romans.

I've included a stone wall and lots of flower beds in this cottage scene. Feel free to add as much color to your flowers as you wish.

Materials

DecoArt Americana Acrylic Paints

Titanium White DA1	Sand DA4	Cadmium Yellow DA10	Boysenberry Pink DA29	Williamsburg Blue DA40	Sea Aqua DA46
Olive Green DA56	Mocha DA60	Burnt Sienna DA63	Burnt Umber DA64	Lamp Black DA67	Slate Grey DA68
French Grey Blue DA98	Sapphire DA99	Dioxazine Purple DA101	Hauser Medium Green DA132	Hauser Dark Green DA133	Yellow Green DA134
Antique Rose DA156	Honey Brown DA163	Light Buttermilk DA164	Golden Straw DA168	Milk Chocolate DA174	Green Mist DA177
Violet Haze DA197	Backlight Mix (Sapphire DA99 + Dioxazine Purple DA101 + a touch of Light Buttermilk DA164)		Walnut Mix (Burnt Umber DA64 + a touch of Lamp Black DA67)		Materials list continued on page 118.

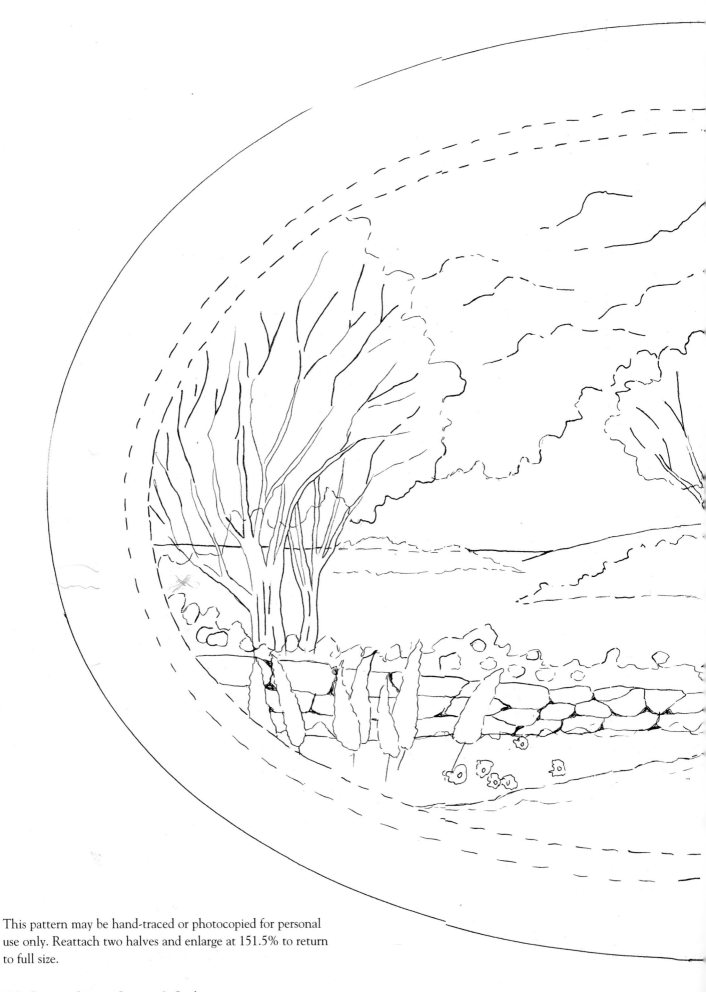

This pattern may be hand-traced or photocopied for personal use only. Reattach two halves and enlarge at 151.5% to return to full size.

Preparation

1. Fill, sand and seal the wood.
2. Base the center oval and the inside routed area with Sand, using your large glazing brush.
3. When this is dry, transfer the pattern for the horizon line, path, house and walls.

Materials continued

Surface

This oval surface comes in three different sizes. I used the medium size. It may be purchased from Roland Nimmo, 9198 Bonita Drive, Cherry Valley, California 92223. Phone (909) 845-6527.

Diane's Angel Series Brushes

- Diane's Angel Mist brush, ⅜-inch (1cm)
- Diane's Angel Hair brush, ⅜-inch (1cm)

Loew-Cornell Brushes

- series 798 ¾-inch (1.9cm) glazing brush
- series 7050 10/0 liner
- series 7400 ½-inch (1.3cm) angle
- series 7500 ½-inch (1.3cm) and no. 6 filberts
- no. 2 Jackie Shaw liner

Miscellaneous

- J.W. etc. Wood Filler
- fine sanding disc
- J.W. etc. First Step Wood Sealer
- tracing paper and pencil
- Chacopaper
- Kemper stylus
- sea sponge
- J.W. etc. Right-Step Satin Varnish

1 Wash in the lawn with a mix of half water and half Green Mist. Wash in the path with Milk Chocolate. Line in the timbers on the house and under the roofline with Burnt Umber. Base the chimney with Slate Grey. Base the front stone wall with one coat of Slate Grey. Working wet-on-wet, use your ½-inch (1.3cm) filbert to scumble in the sky area with Light Buttermilk and Williamsburg Blue. Keep the sky darker at the top of the design and lighter toward the horizon.

2 Tint the sky with washes of Sea Aqua and Antique Rose. When dry, use your angle brush and Sand to float your first layer of clouds on. Highlight just the tops of a few clouds with Light Buttermilk. If your clouds appear a little too yellow, rehighlight with Titanium White.

3 Use your angle brush and Milk Chocolate to shade the sides of the path. Add a second shade on the path with Burnt Umber.

4 Float highlights of Light Buttermilk through the center of the path.

5 Use your ½-inch (1.3cm) filbert brush and the walnut mix to deepen the shadows on your path. The darkest shadows on the path should have touches of Violet Haze to highlight the shadow areas.

6 Tint the path with washes of Olive Green and Boysenberry Pink.

Hint
I prefer to alternate between shadows and highlights when adding color to my painting. This gives each item in the design a more blended look.

7 Use your angle brush and Hauser Dark Green to shade the lawns around the flower beds and on the sides of the scene. Use the chisel edge of your brush to pull shades through the center of the lawn. Add a second shade of Hauser Dark Green plus Burnt Umber in the darkest areas. Highlight through the center of the lawn and on the hill behind the house with Olive Green plus Light Buttermilk. Tint the lawn with Antique Rose.

8 Use your Angel Mist brush to stipple Violet Haze plus water for the trees in the distance. Use your no. 2 liner brush and the walnut mix to line in branches for the trees behind the house.

9 Use your Angel Mist brush to stipple foliage on the trees with Hauser Dark Green, Hauser Medium Green, Hauser Medium Green plus Burnt Sienna and finally Olive Green. Use your angle brush to float a shadow on the trees next to the house using Hauser Dark Green. Repeat with the walnut mix. Highlight just a few tree tips with a stipple of Yellow Green plus Titanium White. Dab in a little of the backlight mix in the darkest areas of the trees. Stipple a little Sea Aqua on the lightest parts of the trees.

10 Use your no. 6 filbert and the wet-on-wet method to paint the remaining tree trunks. This is done with Milk Chocolate, Burnt Umber and Lamp Black. All the large trees on the lawn are painted in the same way. Highlight with a float of Mocha in the lightest areas.

11 Use your Angel Mist brush to stipple in foliage on the trees, using Hauser Dark Green, Hauser Medium Green, Olive Green, and Yellow Green plus Titanium White. Add some backlight mix to the leaves that are in the shadows.

12 Wash the inside of the windows with Williamsburg Blue. Use your 10/0 liner brush to line in the windows with Light Buttermilk. Use your angle brush to shade the walls with Milk Chocolate. Add a second shade on the darker sides of the walls with the walnut mix. Base the door with Milk Chocolate and shade with the walnut mix.

13 Tint the walls of the house with a wash of Antique Rose. Use your angle brush to float some backlight mix on the dark walls of the house.

14 Wash the roof with Honey Brown. Use your Angel Hair brush to create straw on the roof. Begin adding shadows with Burnt Umber. Add water to your brush as you paint.

15 Use your Angel Hair brush to add highlights on the straw with Honey Brown, Burnt Sienna, Golden Straw and Light Buttermilk. Add more shadows on the straw with the walnut mix. Tint the roof in the dark areas with the backlight mix. Tint the light areas with Antique Rose.

16 Paint the stone walls and chimney in the same manner, except the stones on the walls will be more elongated and the ones on the chimney will be more round. Use your no. 2 liner brush and the walnut mix to line in the grout. Use your filbert brush wet-on-wet to put in each stone. This is done with Slate Grey, Mocha and Burnt Umber. Add a few lighter stones with Sand for variety.

17 Use your angle brush to shade the chimney and walls with Burnt Umber. You may need to add a second shade with the walnut mix.

18 Add the backlight mix in the darkest area of the chimney and walls. Tint with washes of Antique Rose and Olive Green. Use your no. 6 filbert.

19 Use your Angel Mist brush to stipple foliage in the flower beds and for the flowers that creep up the side of the house. This is done with Hauser Dark Green and Olive Green. Stipple the flowers wet-on-wet with Antique Rose and Titanium White, Cadmium Yellow and Titanium White, Dioxazine Purple and Titanium White, Yellow Green and Titanium White, Sapphire and Titanium White and Sea Aqua and Titanium White.

20 Stipple the greenery and flowers above and below the wall in the same way as you did the flower beds.

21 Use your angle brush to shade the flower beds in front of the wall with the walnut mix. This will remove any harsh edges of color between the path and the flowers. Add the backlight mix into this shadow area for texture.

22 Use your 10/0 liner brush to add stems for the front flowers and small patches of foreground grass using Hauser Dark Green and Olive Green. Use your 10/0 liner brush to dab in small daisies and sunflowers. Use your Angel Mist brush to stipple in tall blue flowers with Dioxazine Purple, Sapphire and Titanium White. Dot in a few Olive Green centers. Take a look at the whole design and make sure there is enough contrast. You may need to change your tree line so that it has an up-and-down flow. Be sure that everything is tinted sufficiently to reflect the colors of the sky and flowers. Make sure all shadow areas have backlight mix. Finally, base the outer frame of the board with French Grey Blue. While this color is still wet, lightly sponge it with Sand. Put at least two coats of J.W. etc. Right-Step Satin Varnish over the entire board.

Resources

Catalina Cottage
125 N. Aspan #5
Azusa, CA 91702
Phone: (626) 969-4001
Fax: (626) 969-4451
Web site: www.catalina-cottage.com
Ceramichrome Softees.

DecoArt
P.O. Box 327
Stanford, KY 40484
Phone: (606) 365-3193
Fax: (606) 365-9739
E-mail: paint@decoart.com
Web site: www.decoart.com

Delta Technical Coatings, Inc.
2550 Pellissier Place
Whittier, CA 90601
Phone: (800) 423-4135
Fax: (562) 695-5157
Web site: www.deltacrafts.com

Expressive Arts and Crafts
12455 Branford, Unit 6
Arleta, CA 91331
Phone: (800) 747-6880
McCloskey oil sealer, Saral paper and Kemper stylus.

Hofcraft
1730-B Air Park Drive
Grand Haven, MI 49417
Phone: (616) 847-8989
Wicker tray for project nine.

Jo C. and Co.
111 Parrish Lane
Wilmington, DE 19810-3457
Phone: (302) 478-7619
Candy dish for project one.

Loew-Cornell
563 Chestnut Avenue
Teaneck, NJ 07666-2490
Phone: (201) 836-7070
Fax: (201) 836-8110
E-mail:
loew-cornell@loew-cornell.com
Web site: www.loew-cornell.com
Loew-Cornell brushes, tubs and Super Chacopaper.

J. W. etc.
2205 First Street, Suite 103
Simi Valley, CA 93065
Phone: (805) 526-5066
Fax: (805) 526-1297
E-mail: jwetc@earthlink.net
Website: www.jwetc.com

Roland Nimmo
9198 Bonita Drive
Cherry Valley, CA 92223
Phone: (909) 845-6527.
Three-drawer chest for project four and partitioned box for project five (wholesale only).

Stan Brown Arts and Crafts
13435 N.E. Whitaker Way
Portland, OR 97230
Phone: (800) 547-5531.
Small cupboard for project six.

Talk of the Town
9000 Arlington Avenue #102
Riverside, CA 92503
Phone: (909) 687-4160.
Bisque teapot for project three.

The Tole Bridge
1875 Norco Dr.
Norco, CA 91760
Phone: (909) 272-6918
E-mail: tolebridge@aol.com
Web site:
http://members.aol.com/tolebridge/
Diane's Angel Series Brushes, three-drawer chest for project four and partitioned box for project five (retail only).

Valhalla Designs
343 Twin Pines Drive
Glendale, OR 97442
Phone: (541) 832-3260
Mushroom box for project seven.

Index